PENGUIN BOOKS

2041

FAMOUS TRIALS

Edited by James H. Hodge

EIGHTH SERIES

James Hozier Hodge was born in Edinburgh in 1906 and educated at Edinburgh Academy and Edinburgh University. He joined the Auxiliary Air Force in 1930 and served with the R.A.F. during the war, obtaining four mentions in dispatches. He joined William Hodge & Co. Ltd in 1927, and is now chairman of that company and subsidiary printing and shorthand-writing firms. He succeded his father, Harry Hodge, who died in 1947, as general editor of the *Notable British Trials* series and the Penguin *Famous Trials*, and he founded the *War Crimes Trials* series in 1948, which he edited with Sir David Maxwell Fyfe, Q.C. (now Lord Kilmuir). He is married to a graduate of Glasgow School of Art. They live in Edinburgh and have one daughter.

FAMOUS TRIALS

EIGHTH SERIES

———

CAPTAIN WILLIAM KIDD

DR THOMAS SMETHURST

ALFRED ARTHUR ROUSE

PATRICK CARRAHER

JOHN THOMAS STRAFFEN

———

EDITED BY
JAMES H. HODGE

PENGUIN BOOKS

Penguin Books Ltd, Harmondsworth, Middlesex
U.S.A.: Penguin Books Inc., 3300 Clipper Mill Road, Baltimore 11, Md
AUSTRALIA: Penguin Books Pty Ltd, 762 Whitehorse Road,
Mitcham, Victoria

—

First published in the Notable British Trials Series by
William Hodge & Co. Ltd
(*Captain Kidd*, 1930; *Dr Thomas Smethurst*, 1931; *Alfred Arthur Rouse*, 1931;
Patrick Carraher, 1951; *John Thomas Straffen*, 1954)
These abridged versions published in Penguin Books 1963

—

Copyright © James H. Hodge, 1963

—

Made and printed in Great Britain
by Cox & Wyman Ltd
London, Fakenham, and Reading
Set in Intertype Baskerville

Contents

PREFACE   9

CAPTAIN KIDD · 1701   11
By Graham Brooks

DR THOMAS SMETHURST · 1859   66
By L. A. Parry

ALFRED ARTHUR ROUSE · 1931   106
By Helena Normanton

PATRICK CARRAHER · 1938 and 1946   153
By George Blake

JOHN THOMAS STRAFFEN · 1952   182
By Letitia Fairfield and Eric P. Fullbrook

Preface

THE five cases included in the eighth volume of this series could hardly differ more. They span two and a half centuries in time and range from piracy and murder on the high seas to stabbing in the squalid areas of Glasgow. The characters in the dock vary from a professional doctor to a mentally defective labourer, the motives from financial gain to imaginary spite against the police, indeed to practically no motive at all. One man was twice tried for murder; another found unfit to plead on his first arraignment for two murders was convicted at a later date of a third. Crime certainly can provide variety.

Captain Kidd stands high in the list of notorious pirates of the past, but in fact he was a man of considerable ability and standing, with a good record in the service of his country. Unlike so many of his contemporaries, he was no ruffian. He had but one murder and arson against him. He stood charged in four trials, one for murder and three for piracy.

The attention drawn at the time to the trial for murder of Dr Smethurst is not surprising. His first trial had to be abandoned through the illness of a juror. After his conviction there was voluminous correspondence in the Press, especially the medical section, and the Home Secretary of the day took the extraordinary step of consulting an eminent surgeon as to the justice of the verdict. Smethurst was granted a free pardon, and was then tried and convicted of bigamy. Finally he brought a successful action to prove the will of his alleged victim. Surely a most exceptional state of affairs.

The other three essays deal with cases of this century. Rouse was the first person in Britain known to have used a motor-car for committing a murder in order to disappear. Having picked up and given a lift to a man whose origins were never traced, he plied him with drink, probably struck him with a mallet, and then set fire to the car hoping that the charred body would be accepted as his. He was in considerable matrimonial difficulties, and his disappearance and the collection of the insurance money would have been of great value to him at that time. However, he

9

was seen leaving the blazing wreck, and having suddenly to change his plans was in a very short time arrested. Paddy Carraher was a product of the slums of Glasgow, and a very worthless citizen at that. In 1938 he was charged with murder, but on account of drink and provocation got off with a sentence of three years for culpable homicide. After a further conviction for violence in 1943, 1946 found him again in the dock in Glasgow on a capital charge, and this time he was not so fortunate. Paddy's story is typical of the worst section of the sordid side of life to be found in certain, albeit small, sections of Clydeside where shiftlessness and alcoholism abound. He was a man who was almost destined to end his days on the scaffold.

The story of Straffen is unique in British life. A certified high-grade mental defective he thought nothing of strangling little girls, although never violent against anybody else. He left the bodies lying quite openly, and never molested them apart from causing death. In just over two weeks he strangled two children, and being found insane on arraignment was sent to Broadmoor. Six months later he escaped, and within a few hours killed a third small girl. He was arraigned at Winchester Assizes for the third crime, to which he pleaded not guilty, and evidence of the first two crimes was admitted in evidence. Again trouble arose. One of the jurors discussed the case on the first night at a club, and the trial had to start all over again with a fresh jury. Despite a large body of expert medical evidence and his past history, no one could say that he did not know what he was doing nor that it was wrong to do so. Despite his defective mentality he was convicted and sentenced to death, being ultimately reprieved and imprisoned during the Sovereign's pleasure. It was not a popular reprieve, but his Broadmoor escape and the resultant crime led to a full inquiry and changes in the security and alarm system of that Institution.

All five cases are as before taken from the Notable British Trials Series where in individual volumes the reader can study further the full details of the evidence and the additional relative material.

J.H.H.

Captain Kidd

· 1701 ·

BY

GRAHAM BROOKS

THE name of Captain Kidd has been saddled with a degree of infamy far in excess of his deserts. The Kidd of history is but a shadow of the Kidd of legend. True, in middle age, after a successful career of good service, with ample means for a life of respectable retirement, he played the buccaneer; but at worst he was a mere milk-and-water amateur, for, in an age when pirates massacred or enslaved their victims, and sacked and burnt the towns on which they descended for provisions, Kidd had but one murder and one arson to his discredit. His is no romantic story, but the sordid tale of a weak man who succumbed without a struggle when tempta-tion faced him. Yet, whilst the names of such as Morgan, Avery, and Lolonais are scarcely remembered, that of Cap-tain Kidd remains a nursery byword.

If Kidd has suffered at the hands of tradition, he has certainly been too leniently treated by his biographers. Sir Cornelius Dalton in *The Real Captain Kidd* has even gone so far as to depict the pirate as an innocent man of integrity and courage who was the victim of a deliberate travesty of justice. Even the *Dictionary of National Biography* declares that Kidd did not have a fair trial, but was convicted on insufficient evidence. This is an ambiguous statement, for there were four distinct trials, one for murder and three for piracy. As a fact, there was ample evidence in each case upon which the jury could find the prisoner guilty; there was no irregularity in procedure; at each trial the judge summed up with scrupulous fairness on the facts before him;

11

and it is abundantly clear that Kidd was guilty of all the charges preferred against him. It is true that certain aspects of the case do not commend themselves to the modern conscience, but it is clear that they did not result in any miscarriage of justice.

William Kidd was a man of some education. He could write a good letter – no mean achievement in those days. Tradition alleges that his father was a Calvinist minister, who suffered torture by the boot for his faith after the Restoration and died in 1679, but of this there is no proof. Kidd himself was born about the year 1645 at Greenock, then a mere fishing village which ten years previously had secured its Charter as a Burgh of Barony from Charles I. Amongst the fishing-craft there crept up the Clyde occasionally the tall masts of merchantmen. The clank of windlass and capstan, the rhythmic throbbing of the sea-shanties, the creak of sail and anchor, the glint of sun on cutlass and the Babel of foreign tongues – all these brought the tang of the sea to Greenock. Small wonder, then, that young Kidd felt the call and went afloat whilst still a boy.

Of his early career nothing is known. That it was creditable is clear, for on next hearing of Kidd we find him fighting for his country in command of a ship in American waters; that it was successful also may be inferred from the fact that he then owned several trading vessels and considerable property in New York, where he had a wife and children, and where also he was highly respected. War had broken out between England and France immediately after the assumption of the Crown by William of Orange. French privateers were cruising in American waters, and the colonists were ill-protected by English frigates. Kidd at once 'brought his ship from a place that belonged to the Dutch, and brought her into the King's service'. He was thereupon sent by General Codrington to serve under the orders of Colonel Hewson, with whom he fought in two engagements

against the French, and afterwards saw further active service
in the West Indies. His conduct in action was highly
creditable.

Kidd also rendered other good services to William III.
The English Revolution had had its repercussions in the
American colonies; New York, in particular, had been the
scene of much unrest and strife, culminating in the armed
insurrection of Leisler and Milborne. Jacob Leisler, a
German colonist, and his son-in-law, James Milborne,
pretending greater loyalty to the new régime, had seized
Fort James, and had fired upon the troops of Major
Ingoldsby, who had come to demand possession of the fort
in the King's name. Leisler then set himself up as temporary
Governor. On Colonel Sloughter's arrival, both Leisler and
Milborne were convicted of treason, and executed on 16
May 1691. Colonel Henry Sloughter was the new Governor
appointed by the King, and it was thought right that Kidd
should be accorded some official recognition of his services
in the cause of law and order during the period of unrest.

On 18 April 1691, the following resolution was passed by
the Provincial Council of New York:

By His Excellency and Council.

Gabriel Monvile Esq. and Thomas Willet Esq. are appointed
to attend the House of Representatives and acquaint them of the
many good services done to this Province by Captain William
Kidd in his attending here with his vessels before His Excellency's arrival and that it would be acceptable to His Excellency
and the Board that they consider of some suitable reward to him
for his good services.

Accordingly, on the following 14 May the House of
Representatives resolved 'that His Excellency be addressed
unto, to order the Receiver-General to pay to Captain
William Kidd One Hundred and Fifty Pounds current
money of this Province as a suitable reward for the many

...one to this Province'. By this time Kidd's
...r courage and seamanship had spread beyond
...s of his home province, for later in the year the
...ent of the neighbouring colony of Massachusetts
...sioned him to chase an enemy privateer off the coast.

Such, then, was the man who, in 1695, brought one of his
own trading sloops to anchor in the Thames; a typical sea
captain of the age, owner of several vessels, possessed of
sufficient property and means to end his days in comfort with
his family in the colony where he was respected and admired.
That is the William Kidd of 1695. When next he set sail
from England it was upon a voyage which was to bring him
lasting infamy.

To appreciate fully the causes of Kidd's subsequent downfall it is necessary to make a brief survey of the state of
piracy at the close of the seventeenth century, and in particular to consider the state of public opinion with regard to
it in England and the colonies.

*

Right up to the Napoleonic period wars were inevitably
followed by a general aftermath of piracy, partly owing to
the consequent inability of the warring nations to spare
vessels for police purposes, and partly on account of the taste
for freebooting acquired by those who had served as
privateersmen during the period of hostilities. The last few
years of the seventeenth century witnessed a violent revival
of piracy following the sequence of wars in which the three
great naval powers of the period – England, France, and
Holland – had been engaged.

To the Government in London this outburst of piracy
proved embarrassing and difficult; for, whilst the King's
subjects with interests in the East clamoured for its suppression, it was his subjects in America who were chiefly responsible for starting and continuing it. The American

colonies were, indeed, the great breeding ground of buccaneers. The reason is not hard to fathom. Pirates, like other thieves, can thrive at their trade when there is a convenient market for the disposal of their ill-gotten goods. The short-sighted policy of Great Britain in insisting that her colonists should trade exclusively with her – forcing them to buy at the high prices inevitably resulting from such a policy – had made those colonists only too willing to purchase goods cheap from the smugglers or the pirates without asking awkward questions. There was thus a ready-made market that acted like a magnet to the pirates; whilst, as a corollary, there evolved among the American colonists an attitude, not only of toleration, but actually of welcome towards these illicit merchants of cheaper goods -- so much so, that openly-avowed pirates became a recognized and popular element of society in Massachusetts and New York. Moreover, in the American colonies there was no judicial machinery for trying pirates, who consequently found there not only a ready market but also a safe and pleasant home between voyages.

Yet another reason for the popularity of piracy in these colonies was the propinquity of the West Indies. It is not hard to understand why the West Indies Archipelago had become one of the two most profitable hunting-grounds of the pirates; first, it provided so many uninhabited islands abounding with provisions, as lurking-places from which the waiting robbers could watch and pounce upon the unsuspecting merchant vessel; secondly, it lay right on the trade route used by the French, Spanish, Dutch, and English ships across the Atlantic; thirdly, its very nature made pursuit and capture by men-of-war difficult, for the islands abounded in inlets and harbours into which the ships could slip unseen. Here it was, then, that these American pirates found their prey, using the colonies for both market and home between voyages. As time wore on, these men, enriched by the proceeds of their raids, ventured farther afield to that other happy hunting-ground, the richer one in the East Indies, where they could seize and plunder the ships of wealthy 'Moors' trading in the East. All Moslems, Indians, and Armenians were called 'Moors' by sailors.

It must be remembered that at this time Moslems were still universally regarded as the hereditary enemies of Europe. When Darby Mullins, executed at the same time as Kidd for the same offence, told Paul Lorrain, the Newgate Ordinary, that 'he had not known but that it was very lawful to plunder ships and goods belonging to the enemies of Christianity', he was only voicing the belief of the average common seaman of the day. It was this general trend of public opinion that led to many men of standing and ability taking part in the trade of robbing Moors. Thomas Tew was a sea captain of proved worth who had been sent by the Governor of the Bermudas in command of a privateer sloop to capture the French factory at Goory on the Gambian coast; on the voyage he and his crew turned pirate. Robert Culliford was one of the East India Company's most trusted captains; yet he made off with the company's ship in the middle of a voyage in order that he and his crew might make their fortunes by plundering the Moors. No less a person than Colonel Benjamin Fletcher, Governor of New York and Pennsylvania from 1692 to 1696, was dismissed on account of suspicions that he was protecting the pirates for his private gain. It was the participation of such men that rendered the American pirates a menace to the world.

By 1695 the Government in London was deeply concerned for British trade with the East. In that year the East India Company had represented to the Government that the continual depredations of these pirates from America and Madagascar upon the vessels of the Great Mogul were creating imminent danger of reprisals on the company's ships. The company accordingly petitioned that a man-of-war might be dispatched for the specific purpose of wiping out these pirates. The Government gave earnest consideration to this matter, but it was found that there was no suitable vessel which could be spared (England being still at war with France), and that Parliament had so appropriated the money voted for the Admiralty that none could be utilized for the purposes of such an expedition.

William III, therefore, took two steps which were to play a decisive part in the history of William Kidd. First, he appointed Lord Bellomont Governor of New England, with explicit instructions to suppress the growth of piracy in that province and along the American coast; and, secondly, he proposed to his Ministers that the ship requested by the East India Company should be fitted out and dispatched by means of a private undertaking, for which he himself would contribute the sum of £3,000, if the Ministers could raise the balance of whatever sum might be required. The King characteristically quibbled out of his promise to subscribe; but his suggestion bore fruit, for certain prominent persons (headed by Lord Bellomont, who as we have seen was under orders to suppress the American pirates) decided to fit out an expedition themselves.

*

Meanwhile, Kidd had arrived in the Thames with his trading sloop. In London he met an acquaintance from New York, one Colonel Robert Livingston.

Livingston was a man of considerable importance in his native colony. Born in Scotland in 1654, he had emigrated with his father to America at an early age and settled in Albany, where his ability and popularity soon raised him to the positions of town clerk, member (and afterwards Speaker) of the Provincial Assembly, colonel in the Provincial forces, and, owing to his intimate knowledge of the natives, Secretary for Indian Affairs. He was a large landowner in New York and wielded great influence. It was therefore natural that Bellomont, on receiving his appointment as Governor of New England, should consult Livingston, who happened to be in London at the time, and mention to him the orders and suggestions which he had received with regard to the suppression of piracy. Bellomont also spoke of the proposed expedition against the pirates in eastern waters. Livingston, meeting Kidd soon afterwards in London, and remembering that captain's good services to their home province, recommended him to Bellomont as one who could fitly be entrusted with the command of such an expedition.

Kidd was thereupon taken into the confidence of the promoters, and his advice sought as to the choice and purchase of a ship. It was estimated that £6,000 would be required to finance the adventure; Bellomont offered to find four-fifths of this sum, if Kidd and Livingston would find the balance between them; and so, on 10 October 1695, the following document was signed by the three parties concerned:

Articles of Agreement Made This 10th Day of October in the Year of Our Lord 1695 between The Right Honourable Richard Earl of Bellomont of the One Part and Robert Levingston Esq. and Capt. William Kid of the Other Part.

Whereas the said Capt. William Kid is desirous of obtaining a commission as Captain of a Private Man of War in order to take prizes from the King's enemies, and other ways to annoy them, and whereas certain persons did sometime since depart from New England, Rode Island, New York, and other parts in America and elsewhere with an intention to become pirates, and to commit spoils and depredations, against the laws of the nations, in the Red Sea or elsewhere and to return with such goods and riches as they should get to certain places by them agreed upon; of which said persons and places the said Capt. Kid hath notice, and is desirous to fight with and subdue the said Pirates, as also all other Pirates with whom the said Capt. Kid shall meet at sea in case he be empowered so to do. And whereas it is agreed between the said parties That for the purpose of the aforesaid a good and sufficient Ship to the liking of the said Capt. Kid shall be forthwith bought, whereof the said Capt. Kid is to have the command. Now these presents do witness and it is agreed between the said parties,

I That the Earl of Bellomont doth covenant and agree at his proper charge to procure from the King's Majesty or from the Lords Commissioners of the Admiralty (as the case shall require) one or more commissions, empowering him the said Capt. Kid to act against the King's enemies, and to take prizes from them, as a private man of war in the usual manner: and also to fight with, conquer, and subdue pirates and to take them and their goods, with other large and beneficial powers and clauses in such commissions as may be most proper and effectual in such cases.

II The said Earl of Bellomont doth covenant and agree, That within three months after the said Capt. Kid's departure from England, for the purposes in these presents mentioned, he will procure at his proper charge a Grant from the King, to be made to some indifferent and trusty person, of all such merchandizes goods treasure and other things as shall be taken from the said pirates, or any other Pirates whatsoever, by the said Capt. Kid or by the said ship or any other ship or ships under his command.

III The said Earl doth agree to pay four fifths parts, the whole in five parts to be divided, of all moneys which shall be laid out for the buying such good and sufficient ship for the purposes aforesaid, together with rigging and other apparel and Furniture thereof, and providing the same with competent victualling, the said ship to be approved by the said parties; and the said other one fifth part of the charges of the said ship to be paid for by said Robert Levingston and William Kid.

IV The said Earl doth agree, That in order to the speedy buying the said ship, in part of the said four parts of five of the said charges, he will pay down the sum of sixteen hundred pounds by way of advance on or before the sixth day of November next ensuing.

V The said Robert Levingston and William Kid do jointly and

severally covenant and agree That on or before the sixth day of November when the Earl of Bellomont is to pay the said sum of sixteen hundred pounds as aforesaid, they will advance and pay down four hundred pounds in part of the share and proportion which they are to have in the said ship.

VI The said Earl doth agree to pay such further sums of money as shall complete and make up the said four parts of five of the charges of the said ship's apparel, furniture, and victualling, unto the said Robert Levingston and William Kid within seven weeks after the date of these Presents; and in like manner the said Robert Levingston and Capt. Kid do agree to pay such further sums as shall amount to a fifth part of the whole charge of the said ship within seven weeks after the date of these Presents.

VII The said Capt. Kid doth covenant and agree to procure and take with him on board of the said ship one hundred mariners or seamen, or thereabouts, to make what reasonable and convenient speed he can to set out to sea with the said ship, and to sail to such parts or places where he may meet with the said Pirates, and to use his utmost endeavours to meet with subdue and conquer the said Pirates or any other Pirates, and to take from them their goods merchandizes and treasure. Also to take what prizes he can from the King's enemies, and forthwith to make the best of his way to Boston in New England, and that without touching at any other port or harbour whatsoever, or without breaking bulk or diminishing any part of what he shall so take or obtain, on any pretext whatsoever, of which he shall make Oath, in case the same be desired by the said Earl of Bellomont, and there to deliver the same into the hands and possession of the said Earl.

VIII The said Capt. Kid doth agree That the contract and bargain which he will make with his said Ship's-Crew shall be No Purchase No Pay, and not otherwise; and that the share and proportion which his said Ship's-Crew shall by such contract have of such Prizes, goods, merchandizes, and Treasures as he shall take as prize or from Pirates, shall not at the most exceed a fourth part of the same, and shall be less than a fourth in case the same may reasonably and conveniently be agreed upon.

IX The said Robert Levingston and Capt. Kid do jointly and
severally agree with the said Earl of Bellomont, That in case the
said Capt. Kid do not meet with the said Pirates which went‾
from New England, Rode Island, New York and elsewhere as
aforesaid, or do not take from any other Pirates or from the
King's enemies, such goods merchandizes or other things of
value as, being divided as hereinafter is mentioned, shall full.
recompense the said Earl for the moneys by him expended in
buying the said four fifth parts of the said ship and premises,
that they then shall refund and pay to the said Earl of Bellomont the whole money by him to be advanced in Sterling
money or money equivalent thereunto, on or before the five
and twentieth day of March which shall be in the year of our
Lord 1697. (The Danger of the Seas, and of the King's
enemies, and Mortality of the said Capt. Kid always excepted.)
Upon payment whereof the said Robert Levingston and
William Kid are to have the sole Property in the said ship and
furniture and this Indenture to be delivered up to them, with
all other covenants and obligations thereunto belonging.

X It is agreed between the said parties That as well as the goods
merchandize treasure and other things which shall be taken
from the said Pirates, or any Pirates, by the said William Kid,
as also such prizes as shall be by him taken from any of the
King's enemies, shall be divided in manner following, That is
to say, such part as shall be for that purpose agreed upon by
the said Capt. Kid (so far as the same do not in the whole
exceed a fourth part) shall be paid or delivered to the Ship's-
Crew for their use, and the other three parts to be divided
into five equal parts, whereof the said Earl is to have his own
use four full parts and the other fifth is to be equally divided
between the said Robert Levingston and William Kid and is
to be delivered them by the said Earl of Bellomont without
Deduction or Abatement on any pretence whatsoever; But it
is always to be understood that such Prizes as shall be taken
from the King's Enemies are to be lawfully adjudged Prize in
the usual manner before any Division or otherwise inter-
meddling therewith than according to the intent of the said
commission to be granted in that behalf.

XI Lastly it is covenanted and agreed between the said Parties to these presents, That in case the said Capt. Kid do bring to Boston aforesaid, and there deliver to the Earl of Bellomont, goods merchandizes Treasure or Prizes to the value of one hundred thousand Pounds or upwards, which he shall have taken from the said Pirates, or from other Pirates, or from the King's Enemies, that then the ship, which is now speedily to be bought by the said parties, shall be and remain to the sole use and behalf of him the said Capt. William Kid, as a Reward and Gratification for his Good Service therein.

Memorandum

Before the Sealing and Delivery of these Presents it was covenanted and agreed by the said Earl of Bellomont with the said Robert Levingston and Capt. William Kid that the Person to whom the Grant above-mentioned in these Articles shall be made by his Majesty shall within eight days at the most after such grant has been passed by the Great Seal of England, assign and transfer to each of them the said Robert Levingston Esq. and Capt. William Kid respectively, their Heirs and Assigns, one full tenth part (the Ship's-Crew's share proportion being first deducted) of all such goods Treasure or other things as shall be taken by the said Capt. Kid by virtue of such commissions as aforesaid; and the said Grantee shall make such assignment as aforesaid in such manner as by the said Robert Levingston Esq. and Capt. William Kid or their Counsel Learned in the Law shall be reasonably advised and required.

Thus it will be seen that under these articles neither Kidd nor his crew was to have one penny pay unless the ship took a prize; their pay was in fact entirely dependent upon the number of ships they captured. Kidd, moreover, would be liable to pay money to Bellomont if he did not take sufficient prizes to recoup the Earl for the sums he had laid out. It can readily be appreciated that such terms courted disaster. Here was a ship being sent to sea, manned by men whose livelihood depended upon their seizing other ships, the captain coming from a colony where piracy was regarded as a useful profession rather than as a crime.

By the end of November Kidd had found his ship, the *Adventure Galley*, of 287 tons and thirty-four guns. On 4 December she was duly launched at Castle's Yard, Deptford. In the meantime, Bellomont had not been idle. The £4,800 for which he had made himself responsible had been fully subscribed by six persons – Sir John Somers, the Earls of Orford and Romney, the Duke of Shrewsbury, one Edmund Harrison, and himself. These six persons thus became the real promoters of the expedition; and as their conduct was later to raise a storm of indignation in Parliament and throughout the country, it is well to notice who and what they were.

Richard Coote, Earl of Bellomont, was an Irish nobleman of Whig sympathies, who had been Treasurer and Receiver-General to Queen Mary, until she had lost patience with him and dismissed him, recording in her diary – 'I turned him out and was censured for it all, which was no small vexation to me.' Bellomont had next attained notoriety in 1693 by impeaching the Lord Chancellor of Ireland and one of the Irish Lords Justices for high treason, but the House of Commons had rejected the articles of impeachment as groundless. Though appointed Governor of New England in May 1695, and subsequently of New York also, he did not reach his post until nearly three years later. He died in New York on 5 March 1701, two months before Kidd's trial.

Sir John Somers was the most distinguished lawyer in the kingdom. He had acted as junior counsel at the trial of the Seven Bishops and as chairman of the committee which drew up the famous Declaration of Rights. Appointed Solicitor-General in 1689, he had been promoted Attorney-General in 1691, and Lord Keeper two years later. At the time of the promotion of Kidd's expedition Somers was one of the seven Lords Justices to whom the administration of the realm had been entrusted for the period of the King's absence on active service in the Netherlands. He subscribed £1,000 to the venture.

Henry Sidney, Earl of Romney, was the intriguing and licentious uncle of the notorious second Earl of Sunderland. It was Romney who had conveyed to William of Orange at the Hague the invitation to invade his father-in-law's realm, and he had landed with the Prince at Torbay.

Edward Russell, Earl of Orford, had seen considerable service afloat as Admiral during the sea fighting in Charles II's reign. He had taken part in the operation carried out from 1676 to 1682 against the Barbary corsairs in the Mediterranean.

Charles Talbot, Duke of Shrewsbury, was at this time (like Somers) one of the Lords Justices who were acting during the King's absence. Though still a young man – he was born in 1660 – Shrewsbury was regarded as one of the greatest noblemen of the day, King William having dubbed him 'The King of Hearts'.

Edmund Harrison, a prosperous City merchant, was a director of the New East India Company, and, as such, would of course have a personal interest in the suppression of piracy in eastern waters. Harrison was undoubtedly a shrewd man, supervising the selection of the crew for Kidd, and rejecting all Scotsmen and colonists on the ground that their sympathies would probably be with the smugglers and pirates, and that therefore they were not to be relied upon. He was subsequently knighted in 1698.

These, then, were the men who were virtually Kidd's employers. On 10 December 1695, the following warrant was issued by the Admiralty:

By The Commissioners for Executing the Office of
Lord High Admiral of England, Ireland, Etc.

Whereas by Commission under the Great Seal of England bearing Date the 26th Day of June 1689, or any Three or more of us, are required and authorized to grant Commissions unto such Persons as we deem fitly qualified in that behalf for the apprehending seizing and taking such Ships Vessels and Goods belonging to the French King and His Subjects and Inhabitants within the Dominions of the said French King; and such other Ships Vessels and goods as are or shall be liable for confiscation; with other Powers in the said Commission expressed. These are therefore to will and require you forthwith to cause a Commission or Letter of Marque or Reprisal to be issued out of the High Court of Admiralty of England unto Captain William Kidd, Commander of the *Adventure Galley*, Burden 287 Tons, 34 Guns, and 70 men, to set forth in warlike Manner the said ship called the *Adventure Galley* whereof the said Captain William Kidd is Commander, and to apprehend seize and take the Ships Vessels and Goods belonging to the French King or his Subjects or inhabitants within the Dominions of the said French King; and such other Ships Vessels and Goods as are or shall be liable for confiscation; according to the said Commission granted unto us for that Purpose, and certain Articles and Instructions under her late Majesty's Signet and Sign Manual dated the 2nd of May 1693, a Copy whereof remains with you; and according to the Course of the Court of Admiralty and Laws of Nation; And you are therein to insert a Clause, enjoining the said Captain William Kidd to keep an exact journal of his Proceedings; and therein particularly to take notice of all Prizes which shall be taken by him, the Nature of such Prizes, the Time and Place of their being taken, and the Value of them, as near as he can judge; as also the Station, Motion, and Strength of the Enemy, as well as he can discover by the best Intelligence he can get; Of which he is, from time to time, as he shall have an Opportunity, to transmit an Account for us to our Secretary, and to keep a Correspondence with him by all Opportunities that shall present; Provided always, That, before you issue such Commission, Security be given thereupon, according as directed in her late Majesty's Instructions afore-mentioned; as also, That a Recognizance, or sufficient security, not exceeding 500 *l.* be entered into, obliging him not to carry in the said Ship more than one half of her Complement of Seamen but that all the rest of her Company be Landmen; and that he do, at the end of the Voyage, give in to the

Secretary of the Admiralty a perfect List, in Columns, of his Ship's Company, expressing their Names, Qualities, Age, Place of Abode, and whether married or single Men; and also, That he do give security strictly to conform himself to the Regulations contained in their Majesties' Proclamation of the 12th of July, 1694, concerning Colours to be worn on board Ships. This to continue in force till further Order; for which this shall be your Warrant.

Given under our Hands and the Seal of the Office of Admiralty, this Tenth Day of December, 1695.

> F. Lowther
> H. Preistman
> H. Rich

To Sir Charles Hedges, Knight
  Judge of the High Court of Admiralty of England
By Command of the Commissioners   Wm Bridgman

A Commission in the terms directed in the above warrant was issued accordingly to Kidd the following day, and on 26 January 1696 the Great Seal was affixed to a second commission, by which Kidd was authorized to apprehend and seize four specified pirates, and any other pirates, freebooters, or sea-rovers whom he might find:

William The Third, by the Grace of God, King of England, Scotland, France and Ireland, Defender of the Faith. To our Trusty and well-beloved Captain William Kidd, Commander of the Ship *Adventure Galley*, or to the Commander of the said Ship for the time being; Greeting. Whereas we are informed, That Captain Thomas Too, John Ireland, Captain Thomas Wake, Captain William Maze or Mace, And other of our Subjects, Natives or Inhabitants of New England, New York, and elsewhere in our Plantations in America, have associated themselves with divers other wicked and ill-disposed persons; and do against the Laws of Nations, daily commit many great Piracies, Robberies, and Depridations, upon the Seas in the Parts of America and in other Parts, to the great Hindrance and Discouragement of Trade and Navigation, and to the Danger and

Hurt of our loving Subjects, our Allies, and all others, navigating the Seas, upon their lawful Occasions; Now know ye, That we, being desirous to prevent the aforesaid Mischiefs, and, as far as in us lies, to bring the said Pirates, Free-booters, and Sea Rovers, to Justice, have thought fit, and do hereby give and grant unto you, the said William Kidd to whom our Commissioners for executing the Office of our Lord High Admiral have granted a Commission as a private Man of War, bearing date the Eleventh Day of December, 1695; and unto the Officers, Mariners and others, which shall be under your Command, full power and Authority to apprehend seize and take into your custody as well the said Captain Tho. Too, John Ireland, Captain Thomas Wake, William Maze alias Mace, as such Pirates, Free-booters, and Sea-Rovers, being either our own Subjects or of other Nations associated with them, which you shall meet upon the said Coasts or Seas of America, or in any other Seas or Parts, with their Ships and Vessels; And also such Merchandizes, Money, Goods, and Wares, as shall be found on board, or with them, in case they shall willingly yield themselves, but if they will not submit without fighting, then you are by Force to compel them to yield: And we do also require you to bring, or cause to be brought, such Pirates, Free-booters and Sea Rovers, as you shall seize, to a legal Tryal, to the end they may be proceeded against according to the law in such cases: And we do hereby charge and command all our Officers, Ministers, and other our loving Subjects whatsoever, to be aiding and assisting to you in the Premises; And we do hereby enjoin you to keep an exact journal of your Proceedings in the execution of the Premises; and therein to set down the Names of such Pirates, and of their Officers and Company, and the Names of such Ships and Vessels, as you shall, by virtue of these Presents, seize and take; and the Quantities of Arms, Ammunition, Provision, and Loading of such Ships, and the true value of the same, as near as you can judge: And we do hereby jointly charge and Command you, as you will answer the same at your utmost Peril, That you do not, in any manner, offend or molest any of our Friends and Allies, their Ships or Subjects, by Colour or Pretence of these Presents, or the Authority hereby granted. In Witness thereof, we have caused our Great

Seal of England to be affixed to the Presents. Given at our Court at Kensington, the 26th Day of January, 1695/6, in the Seventh Year of our Reign.

Thus by the end of January Kidd was in possession of his ship and two commissions. As security for the due performance of his obligations he was required to enter into a bond for £20,000 and Colonel Livingston was required also to enter into another bond for £10,000 as guarantor of Kidd's integrity. There now remained but one thing to be obtained – the most important thing of all, from the point of view of Bellomont and Kidd – namely, the right to retain the profits of the expedition. So anxious was the King that the East India Company's request for a ship should be met that Bellomont experienced little difficulty in obtaining the required concession; a document was drawn up, whereby the King, in consideration of the fitting out of the expedition, granted to the promoters thereof all such ships and goods as might be taken by Kidd from any pirates he might find in pursuance of his commission. Bellomont and Harrison were named therein as two of the grantees, but so anxious were the other lords to keep their connexion with the undertaking from public knowledge that the names of four dummy grantees were inserted in lieu of their own names.

On 25 February 1696 Kidd received his sailing orders from Bellomont:

Captain William Kidd:
You being now ready to sail, I do hereby desire and direct you that you and your Men do serve God in the best Manner you can: That you keep good Order, and good Government in your Ship: That you make the best of your Way to the Place and Station where you are to put the Powers you have in Execution, and, having effected the same, You are, according to Agreement, to sail directly to Boston in New England, there to deliver unto me the whole of what Prizes, Treasure, Merchandizes, and other Things, you shall have taken by virtue of the Powers and

Authorities granted you : But if, after the Success of your Design, you shall fall in with any English Fleet bound for England, having good convoy, you are in such case to keep them company, and bring your Prizes to London, notwithstanding any Covenant to the contrary in our Articles of Agreement. Pray fail not to give Advice, by all Opportunities, how the Galley proves; how your Men stand, what Progress you make; and in general, of all remarkable Passages in your Voyage, to the time of your Writing. Direct your letters to Mr Edmund Harrison.

I pray God grant you good Success, and send us a good Meeting again.

Bellomont

And so, two days later, Kidd weighed anchor at Deptford in the *Adventure Galley*.

*

According to Kidd's own narrative, the *Adventure Galley* was stopped at the Nore on 1 March and held up there for nineteen days, while some of his crew were pressed for the fleet. On the face of it, this would appear improbable, for the crews of privateers were regarded as exempt from impressment; yet, there is no other reason to doubt this statement, for Kidd's account of his movements for the first twelve months of the voyage remains uncontradicted in any material particular and is corroborated in many details by the testimony of others. In view of the fact that, on arrival at New York, Kidd undoubtedly did have to recruit a substantial addition to his crew, the balance of probability is that his statement with regard to the impressment at the Nore is correct.

When allowed to proceed once more, Kidd made for the Downs with the eighty men left to him – one must assume that they were not the pick of the original strength, who would undoubtedly have been the ones 'pressed' – called at Plymouth, and finally set sail for the New World on 23 April

1696. During May Kidd took a small French vessel, bound for Newfoundland with salt and fishing-tackle, and on his arrival at New York on 4 July she was condemned as a lawful prize, her cargo sold, and the proceeds expended in laying in a further stock of provisions for the *Adventure Galley*.

In New York Kidd set about filling the vacancies created by the impressment of his men at the Nore, and brought the strength of his crew up to 155. That he should have been forced to recruit men, for the purpose of this voyage, in a colony where piracy was prevalent, was at the least highly unfortunate. If none was an actual pirate, many must have had piratic sympathies. Back in London, shrewd Edmund Harrison had supervised the selection of the crew with such canny care; it was perhaps a mercy that he did not know that all his precautions had been in vain.

There can be little doubt that when Kidd sailed on 6 September 1696 from New York the germs of disaster had already been shipped aboard the *Adventure Galley*.

Crossing the Atlantic, he put into Madeira for fruit and wine on 8 October, and eleven days later he made the Cape Verde Islands, calling at Bonavista (Boa Vista) for salt and at St Jago (São Thiago) for water. At the end of the month he set sail for the Cape of Good Hope, and on 12 December, just before rounding the Cape, he met with four men-of-war under the command of Captain Warren, in whose company he sailed for a week. Making for the western coast of Madagascar, Kidd took the *Adventure Galley* into the port of Telere (Tuliar).

One point here is worthy of note, for it may tend to disclose the direction in which Kidd's thoughts and intentions were already veering. Madagascar was the most notorious stronghold of the pirates in Eastern waters. Kidd had been sent specifically to attack and apprehend these pirates. Might he not then have been reasonably expected – if he were honest in his intentions – to sail up that part of the coast of Madagascar where those pirates were known to lurk, namely, the western coast? Instead of that, we find him avoiding that coast – in fact, he does not go near it for another fifteen months! This fact may, or may not, be significant. On the face of it, it would seem that he had already decided not to appear in these waters as the foe of pirates.

On 4 February 1697 Kidd weighed anchor once more, and, setting a nor'-nor'-westerly course, made for Johanna (Anjuan), an island some 150 miles away, where he watered, and thence to Mihelia (Mohila), where he careened the ship, and where, he states, some fifty of his crew died within a week, probably of cholera. It is at this point that Kidd's own narrative becomes untrustworthy, for it entirely omits any mention of the next important episode – which, however, undoubtedly took place. From now on Kidd records only those events which he believes are not incriminating. It is therefore not unreasonable to assume that it was at this stage that Kidd definitely decided to sacrifice reputation and position for the shadowy fortune to be wrung from robbing Moors.

*

In fairness to Kidd it must be remembered that he was undoubtedly placed in an extremely unenviable position. By the terms of his agreement with Lord Bellomont, neither he nor his crew were entitled to any pay; it was by now more than twelve months since the *Adventure Galley* had left London, and, with the exception of the small French vessel captured *en route* to America (from the proceeds of which none of them had derived any personal benefit) no prize had been taken, and consequently not a penny earned. To make matters worse, sickness had just carried off a third of the crew, and the ship was beginning to leak. It is therefore not surprising that the ship's company had reached a state of rampant discontent, and that from those who had been recruited in New York came open suggestions of piracy as the only means of improving their unhappy lot. Doubtless Kidd found his crew already beyond control. These considerations must be borne in mind when passing judgement on Kidd.

In July 1697 the *Adventure Galley* dropped anchor off Bab's Key, an islet in the mouth of the Red Sea, which served as an admirable lurking-place from which a watch could be kept upon all vessels going in and out of the sea. For three weeks Kidd waited there for the Mocha fleet to come out. Three times he sent a boat through the strait to Mocha to ascertain what the ships were doing. At last, on 14 August the fleet came by. The evidence is conflicting as to who was the aggressor, but shots were undoubtedly exchanged between some of the ships and Kidd, who, realizing that his opponents were numerically too strong for him, made away and set sail for the Malabar coast.

On 20 September when fifteen leagues from Carrawar (Karwar), the *Adventure Galley* met with a Moorish ketch, manned by Moors under an English captain named Parker, with one other European, a Portuguese, on board. Kidd took several bales of paper, several bales of coffee, and some myrrh off the ship. He was, however, unable to find any money and ordered some of the crew to be lashed to the masts and drubbed with naked cutlasses in the hope of making them disclose its whereabouts. Having failed to extract any information, he let the ship go, keeping Parker and the Portuguese on board the *Adventure Galley*. The Portuguese was apparently retained for future use as 'Linguister' – the seaman's name for an interpreter. Kidd then made for Carrawar to wood and water. At Carrawar two of his crew left him, because, so they reported, 'he was going upon an ill design of piracy'. Shortly afterwards some officials from the English factory came aboard to ask if Kidd had got Parker and the Portuguese on the ship; but Kidd stoutly denied their presence (they were hidden in the hold), and put to sea again.

Sailing down the coast, he was attacked by a Portuguese frigate, which he drove off after a long fight, eleven of the crew of the *Adventure Galley* being wounded during the action. Kidd then anchored off one of the islands that fringe the coast and sent a party ashore for water. Some of the natives proved hostile and cut the cooper's throat, whereupon Kidd had one of them tied to a tree and shot, and ordered some of the huts to be set on fire by way of reprisal. Standing out to sea again, Kidd met with a Dutch ship, the *Loyal Captain*, commanded by Captain Hoar. Some of the crew were in favour of taking this ship, but Kidd prevented them. There is reason to believe that, so far, Kidd's evil actions had been due to weakness in submitting to the demands of an unruly crew rather than to malice aforethought. On this occasion he was apparently strong enough to resist them. There was a mild sort of mutiny, which he quelled, but bad feeling continued to run through the ship. Matters came to a head about a fortnight later, on 30 October 1697. William Moore, the gunner, was at work on deck, when Kidd chided him with having wished to take the *Loyal Captain*. Moore denied the charge, whereupon the captain called him 'a lousy dog'. 'If I am a lousy dog,' retorted the gunner, 'then you have made me one.' Kidd paced angrily up and down the deck for a moment or two, then picked up an iron-bound bucket and struck Moore so savagely on the head with it that the gunner died the next day.

It may well be that Kidd felt that by this act of murder he had burnt his boats. He would now no longer sail the seas as a guiltless captain; he had definitely sunk into crime, and he might now just as well be hung for a sheep as for a lamb. Be that as it may, his career of definite piracy now begins. On 27 November, when four leagues from Calicut, he sighted a ship. Hoisting French colours, Kidd gave chase. On coming up with his prey, he found her to be the *Maiden*, a ship of 200 tons, bound for Surat with a cargo of two horses, ten or twelve bales of cotton, some quilts, and sugar. The master, a Dutchman named Mitchell, with two other Dutchmen and eight or nine Moors, came aboard the *Adventure Galley* and declared that it was a Moorish ship, producing a French pass. Kidd put the Moors in the long-boat, sold the cotton and horses on the coast to the natives for money and gold, and took the ship along with him as a prize.

On 28 December, whilst again cruising in the same waters, Kidd seized a Moorish ketch, from which he took some tubs of sugar candy and some tobacco. Twelve days later he stopped a Portuguese vessel, from which he took a quantity of East India goods, some opium, powder, rice, iron, bees-wax, and thirty jars of butter. Sailing inshore, he sold the opium on the coast, and put to sea again, just in time to catch another Portuguese ship on 20 January. He made her also a prize, but was forced to let her go a week later, on being chased by a squadron of Dutch ships.

It was on 30 January 1698 that Kidd took his richest prize, the ship which was to bring about his final downfall. This was the *Quedagh Merchant* (sometimes referred to as the *Kara Merchant* or *Quidah Merchant*), a merchantman of 400 to 500 tons, bound for Surat from Bengal, captured by him about ten leagues from Cochin on the Malabar coast. On sighting her, Kidd gave chase, flying French colours. After four hours he came up with her, and put two shots across her bow. The *Quedagh Merchant* was flying Armenian colours, belonged to Armenian owners, and was commanded by an Englishman named Wright, who (quite naturally, seeing that Kidd was flying French colours) pro-duced a French pass. Kidd thereupon put Captain Wright and his crew (consisting of two Dutchmen, a Frenchman, six or seven Armenians and ninety Moors) into the long-boats, and sent them ashore; and carried off the *Quedagh Merchant* as a prize. She was richly laden with bales of silks and muslins, sugar, iron, saltpetre, guns, and some gold in specie. Some of the goods he sold on the coast for seven or eight thousand pounds. Finding himself now with two prizes – the *Maiden* and the *Quedagh Merchant* – Kidd decided to convoy them to Madagascar. But his latest exploit began to frighten him, and four or five days afterwards he assembled his crew and proposed that they should take back the *Quedagh Merchant* and hand it over to Captain Wright, as 'the taking of this ship would make a great noise in England, and they would not know what to do with the goods taken from the same'; but the crew would not hear of such a thing, and the *Adventure Galley* continued on her course with her two prizes. Whilst still off the southern part of the Malabar coast, he met with another Portuguese ship, and began to plunder her, but was forced to let her go and make his own escape with the two prizes, on sighting men-of-war on the starboard beam, taking with him the ship's master-merchant and seven of the crew who had been taken on board the *Adventure Galley*.

So, in May 1698, Kidd arrived at Madagascar. It is significant that this time he chose that part of the coast which was known to be the haunt of pirates. He dropped anchor at St Marie, an islet off the western coast.

*

Kidd had reached St Marie in the *Adventure Galley*, together with the *Maiden*, some days ahead of the *Quedagh Merchant*. The *Adventure Galley* had become so crazy and leaky that he decided to scrap her; so, after unlading her, he ordered his men to set her on fire. The *Maiden* was scuttled and sunk in St Marie harbour, after everything of use or value had been taken off her. Kidd then proceeded to share the spoils with his men. The bales of silks and muslins and other merchandise in the *Quedagh Merchant* were counted and divided into shares, each share being represented by three or four bales and an odd assortment of other goods. Kidd took forty shares for himself, the rest being divided among the hundred and fifteen members of the crew which had now become depleted. Provisions and stores were bought with the proceeds of the sale of other spoils, and the remainder of the plunder was stored on board the *Quedagh Merchant*.

At St Marie lay another ship. Once she had been the East India Company's *Resolution*, but her captain, Robert Culliford, had run away with her and her crew to turn pirate; now, renamed by him, she was known as the *Mocha Frigate*. On the arrival of Kidd with his ships, Culliford's men (numbering about forty) had run into the woods, thinking that he had come to take them. Exactly what happened after that is uncertain; Kidd's story was that he had endeavoured to persuade his men to capture Culliford and his crew and to take the *Mocha Frigate*, but that they had refused, that ninety of them had deserted him, robbed his ships, and joined Culliford, and that for weeks he had gone in fear of his life, locked in his cabin; on the other hand, against him was the fact that he and Culliford fraternized from the outset. What is certain is that some of Kidd's men did in fact join Culliford, either by agreement with Kidd or otherwise, that Culliford and Kidd went aboard each other's ships, and that eventually Kidd agreed over a drink that he would not molest Culliford or his men in any way.

In view of Kidd's subsequent protestations of innocence, it is well to examine his conduct at Madagascar. Let us assume in his favour for the moment that, as he contended, he had only seized ships which he lawfully might seize. Let us likewise assume that, as he alleged, he in fact endeavoured to persuade his crew to take Culliford and the *Mocha Frigate*. How does his subsequent conduct appear? By the terms of the articles of agreement with Bellomont, and by the terms of his commissions, he was bound to do certain things. Did he honestly attempt to do them? He was bound 'forthwith to make the best of his way to Boston in New England' with his prizes, 'and that without touching at any other port or harbour whatsoever, or without breaking bulk or diminishing any part of what he shall so take or obtain'. He acted in every way contrary to these orders; instead of making for Boston, he put into port at St Marie; instead of taking his prizes home, he destroyed one of them; instead of preserving the cargo, he divided it up between himself and his crew. Even allowing for the fact that his crew was probably so unruly that he could only keep them under control by making them some payment – even then, why did he remain at St Marie for five long months, and why did he not make an inventory of all the captured goods and merchandise as he was bound to do? Moreover, by the articles of agreement, he was strictly bound not to divide any spoils until the ships had been lawfully adjudged prizes.

Three or four weeks after Kidd's arrival, Culliford and one hundred and thirty men sailed away in the *Mocha Frigate*. Kidd remained on at St Marie, bartering goods for money and gold in Madagascar, and recruiting men for his depleted crew. As an example of the type of men with whom Kidd was now amicably associating, one may be mentioned – Captain John Kelly, a notorious pirate, who was afterwards hanged for his many misdeeds in August 1700, the very type of man whom Kidd was ordered to seize. Kelly eventually sailed home with Kidd on the *Quedagh Merchant*.

At last, in September 1698, Kidd set sail, his ship loaded with a rich hoard of merchandise, jewels, gold, and pieces of eight. After a quiet voyage he arrived off Anguilla, in the

West Indies, at the end of April 1699. There he sent some men ashore, where they received the tidings that Kidd and all his crew had been proclaimed pirates.

*

What had been happening meanwhile in England?

Kidd's expedition, it will be remembered, had originated in the King's desire for some response to the East India Company's petition with regard to the suppression of piracy in the Indian seas. Kidd had sailed early in 1696, and the company had not unreasonably hoped for definite results to become apparent towards the end of the year. Matters, however, continued to grow steadily worse; right through 1696 and 1697 the company received report after report of further depredations of the pirates on ships of the Great Mogul, and of the anger consequently aroused amongst the natives, who had in some cases made reprisals on the company's property, seizing its factories and making prisoners of the factors. To make matters even worse came the news that one of the company's own captains – Culliford – had run away with the East Indiaman under his command to join the pirates. The situation was, in fact, becoming desperate; neither on sea nor on land was the company's property safe, and both trade and credit were suffering accordingly. And still the long-awaited news of Captain Kidd did not come. When, at last, tidings did arrive, they were to the effect that he too had turned pirate.

It has already been noted that at Carrawar, in the autumn of 1697, two of Kidd's crew had left him on account of his 'ill design of piracy', and had been arrested and sent home to England for examination at the Admiralty. The cat had thus been let out of the bag at this early date, and the English factories on the western coast of India had soon afterwards learnt of Kidd's other acts of piracy; yet the company in London received no news of this until August 1698, in a

letter from their president at Surat. Then further information came through, including a report that Kidd was at St
Marie, and was intending to sail to the West Indies to refit
prior to returning for further piracies in the Indian seas.

On 18 November 1698 the company wrote to the Lords
Justices, definitely accusing Kidd of piracy in the case of the
seizure of the *Quedagh Merchant*. The Lords Justices at
once took vigorous steps. A squadron had already been
fitted out, in response to the company's many recent complaints, for the suppression of piracy in the East Indies. Its
commander, Captain Warren, then about to sail, was
ordered to 'pursue and seize Kidd if he continue still in
those parts', and also to apprehend Captain Wright (the
skipper of the *Quedagh Merchant*), in order that inquiry
might be made as to how the latter came to surrender his
ship to Kidd without making any resistance. On 23 November a circular letter was dispatched by Rear-Admiral
Benbow to the Governor of every American colony, calling
upon each of them to 'give strict orders and take particular
care for apprehending the said Kidd and his accomplices
wherever he shall arrive . . . as likewise to secure his ships
and all the effects therein, it being Their Excellencies' intention that right be done to those who have been injured
and robbed by the said Kidd, and that he and his associates
be prosecuted with the utmost vigour of the law'. Finally, to
facilitate Kidd's capture, a proclamation was drawn up,
offering a free pardon to all pirates at Madagascar, except-
ing Kidd and two others specifically named, who might
surrender themselves by a specified date to any of the persons
named in the proclamation.

The public soon got wind of these developments, and the
whole country seethed with the wildest rumours. Some of
these rumours were undoubtedly fostered by the political
enemies of Somers (who was then Lord Chancellor) and
Shrewsbury, and the part played by these two lords and their

colleagues in promoting the expedition became the subject of the wildest conjecture – and censure; it was even asserted that the four lords (two of whom were then acting as Lords Justices) had sent Kidd to sea in the *Adventure Galley* with express orders to commit piracy for their benefit, and that to this end they had naturally taken pains to select a captain with great experience of the art of piracy. Even the King was not held above suspicion. During the ensuing summer many canards were spread regarding the fate of the now notorious Kidd. Luttrell, who had a keen relish for such tit-bits of gossip, records some of them:

1 Aug. 1699. We have a report that Captain Kidd who some time since turned pyrate in the *Adventure Galley* and took from the subjects of the Great Mogull and others to the value of £400,000 is taken prisoner by a French ship, the commander of which sent him in irons to the Great Mogull.

3 Aug. 1699. We now have letters from the West Indies which contradict the taking of Captain Kidd the pyrate, and say that after the *Adventure Galley* was sunk he went on board a Portuguese and sailed directly for Darien where the Scots received him and all his riches.

5 Aug. 1699. Captain Kidd the pyrate, some time since said to be taken by a French man-of-war, afterwards contradicted and that he was gone to Darien, we now hear was at Nassau Island, near New York, and sent for Mr Livingstone, one of the Council there, to come aboard; accordingly he went to him and he proffered £30,000 to give the owners, who first fitted out the *Adventure Galley*, and £20,000 for his pardon: but tis presumed the same will not be accepted.

17 Aug. 1699. Letters from Curassau (Curaçao) say that the famous pyrate Captain Kidd in a ship of 30 guns and 250 men offered the Dutch Governor of St Thomas 45,000 pieces of eight in gold and a great present of goods if he would protect him for a month, which he refused: but the said pyrate bought afterwards of an English ship provisions to the value of 25,000 crowns and since supplyed with necessaries from other ships.

22 Aug. 1699. There are letters which say the famous Captain Kidd has surrendered himself to the Lord Bellomont, Governor of New England.

This last rumour proved true. But even the certain knowledge that Kidd was under arrest did not entirely allay the scare which had spread the length and breadth of England. Four powerful lords were known to have been connected with the venture; the public was apprehensive lest these lords should intrigue Kidd's escape, in order that their own culpability might not be brought to light. A small incident was to show how deep-rooted was this suspicion. In September 1699, H.M.S. *Rochester* was ordered to New York to fetch back Kidd in irons. After battling with the elements for some weeks, she crept back, battered, to port for repairs. Immediately a violent public outcry burst forth. This return of the *Rochester*, it was openly alleged, was but a trick of the four great lords to prevent Kidd being brought to England for trial! So great was the uproar and so insistent the allegations that the Lords Justices ordered an official inquiry into the return of the *Rochester*. The inquiry was conducted by Mr St Loe, the Admiralty Commissioner at Plymouth, who reported that Captain Ellis, commander of the *Rochester*, had only done his duty in returning to port; but the public was not altogether satisfied.

The East India Company also apparently had fears that the Government might hush the matter up, unless stirred to action by outside pressure. Accordingly, on 21 September 1699 a deputation from the board of the company waited upon the Lords Justices and presented a petition praying that Kidd be brought to a speedy trial, and that all the goods and effects taken by him from subjects of the Great Mogul be sent back to them.

The House of Commons now decided to inquire into the matter, and called for copies of all documents relating to Kidd's expedition. Accordingly, on 2 December 1699, Mr

Lowndes delivered at the table of the House copies of the commissions to Kidd and of the grant of pirates' goods to Bellomont and the nominees of the four great lords. These documents were read and the House adjourned. Under date 16 March 1700 the following minute appears in the Journal of the House of Commons (volume xiii):

The House being informed that Captain Kidd is sent home from the West Indies,

Resolved. That an humble Address be presented to his Majesty that the said Captain Kidd may not be tried, discharged, or pardoned, until the next session of Parliament. And that the Earl of Bellomont, governor of New England, may transmit over all communications, instructions, and other papers, taken with, or relating to, the said Captain Kidd.

There is little doubt that this address was prompted by the fear that while Parliament was not sitting the four great lords would succeed in securing the release or pardon of Kidd without trial or inquiry. Furthermore, the House was anxious to have Kidd brought before it in person, in order that he might be examined at the bar, in the hope of extracting from him incriminating evidence against the four lords. On 8 April Mr Secretary Vernon acquainted the House that the King, having heard that the ship with Kidd on board had arrived off Lundy Island and was bound for the Downs, had sent his yacht to meet the prisoner, and had given instructions for the Lords of the Admiralty to dispatch their marshal to take him into custody. Still apprehensive, certain members introduced a motion that an address be presented to the King to have Somers removed from the Woolsack 'for ever'; but the motion was defeated by a narrow margin, and the House rose on the day before that on which Kidd arrived in the Thames, a prisoner on the King's yacht.

*

To return to Kidd himself. Having learnt at Anguilla in April 1699 that they had been proclaimed pirates, he and his men, he says, were caused 'great consternation'. They accordingly made for the island of St Thomas, where they were greeted with the same news. Kidd himself says that at St Thomas his brother-in-law, Samuel Bradley, who was sick, was put on shore, and that five others deserted the ship; it is far more probable that the evidence of one of his crew is more reliable in stating that the Governor refused to allow any of them to land. It is certain that the *Quedagh Merchant* made sail as fast as possible from St Thomas. When off the south-western extremity of Porto Rico Kidd spoke the *Antonio*, a trading sloop belonging to a merchant named Boulton, of Antigua. Boulton went on board the *Quedagh Merchant*, and the two ships made together for the island of Mona, between Porto Rico and San Domingo. Boulton was soon persuaded to supply Kidd with provisions; handing over a small supply for immediate needs, Boulton set sail for Antigua, leaving the *Quedagh Merchant* anchored off Mona. Eight days later he returned in the *Antonio* with a large store of provisions, which he sold to Kidd, telling him that a further supply would soon arrive in a brigantine belonging to one Burt. While waiting for this brigantine, the *Quedagh Merchant* broke her moorings in a storm and was blown out to sea, Boulton being on board. The *Antonio* followed, and the two ships and the brigantine, which encountered them at sea, eventually anchored off the coast of Hispaniola (Haiti).

Once again Kidd's conduct was hardly consistent with his pretended innocence. After some negotiations he purchased the *Antonio* from Boulton, payment being made in bales of goods and merchandise from the *Quedagh Merchant*. Some more bales of goods were then sold to the master of the brigantine; others to the captain of a Dutch ship which stood in shore to speak with them; some were transferred into the

Antonio. Leaving the *Quedagh Merchant*, with the remainder (and bulk) of the goods and merchandise on board, in charge of Boulton and twenty-two men, Kidd put to sea in the *Antonio* and made for New England. The arrangement was that Boulton was to wait with the *Quedagh Merchant* at Hispaniola for three months or until Kidd returned, whichever was the shorter period, and he was authorized to sell the goods left on board.

Early in June the *Antonio* ran into Delaware Bay and anchored off Lewiston, where a man named Gillam was landed with a heavy chest. Rounding the east end of Long Island, Kidd ran up the sound into Oyster Bay, whence he dispatched a letter to one Emmot, an old friend of his in New York, requesting him to come on board at once.

Kidd had apparently sailed for New England from Hispaniola with the intention of staking everything upon a game of bluff. Proclaimed pirate as he was, with a squadron out in search of him, he realized that to stay at sea could only mean certain disaster; by returning voluntarily, posing as an innocent man, and handing over some of his ill-gotten spoils, he might still hope to save his neck – it was his only chance. But, on reaching New England, his courage failed him; hence his decision to send Emmot to Bellomont to plead his cause and find out how matters stood. His choice of an ambassador was singularly unfortunate, for Emmot, a lawyer by profession, was an avowed Jacobite and a friend of Colonel Benjamin Fletcher, Bellomont's predecessor in the office of Governor, who had been removed on account of suspected sympathies with the pirates. Emmot came quickly in response to Kidd's summons, boarded the *Antonio* at Oyster Bay, and was landed again at Rhode Island, whence he hastened to Bellomont, whom he interviewed at Boston late at night on 13 June. The nature of that interview will appear hereafter. Bellomont thereupon instructed Mr Duncan Campbell, the postmaster of Boston, to accompany Emmot back to Kidd to persuade him to bring the *Antonio* into port. Emmot and Campbell found Kidd at Block Island, and a long interview took place, after which Campbell returned to Bellomont, to whom, in the presence of the Council, he reported what had transpired.

The nature of the negotiations which had so far taken place, and the nature of the story put forward by Kidd as his defence, are best described by quoting the letter which Bellomont sent to Kidd on 19 June by Duncan Campbell:

Boston, 19 June 1699

Captain Kidd

Mr Emmot came to me last Tuesday Night late, telling me, He came from you, but was shy of telling me where he parted with you; nor did I press him to it; He told me, You came to Oyster Bay, in Nassau Island, and sent for him to New York. He proposed to me, That I would grant you a Pardon: I answered, That I had never granted one yet; and that I had set myself a Rule, not to grant a Pardon to any body whatever without the King's express Leave of Command. He told me, You declared and protested your Innocence; and that, if your Men could be persuaded to follow your Example, you would make no manner of Scruple of coming into this Port, or any other within his Majesty's Dominions: That you owned there were Two Ships taken; but that your Men did it violently against your Will; and had used you barbarously, in imprisoning you, and treating you ill, most Part of the Voyage, and often attempting to murder you. Mr Emmot delivered me Two French Passes, taken on board the Ships which your Men rifled; which Passes I have in my Custody; and I am apt to believe they will be a good Article to justify you, if the late Peace were not, by the Treaty between England and France, to operate in that Part of the World at the time the Hostility was committed, as I am almost confident it was not to do. Mr Emmot also told me, You had about the value of 10,000 *l.* in the Sloop with you; and that you have left a Ship somewhere off the Coast of Hispaniola, in which there was to the Value of 30,000 *l.* more, which you had left in safe Hands, and had promised to go to your People in that Ship, within three

45

Months, to fetch them with you to a safe Harbour. These are all the material Particulars I can recollect that passed between Mr Emmot and me: Only this, That he told me, that you showed a great Sense of Honour and Justice, in professing, with many Asseverations, your settled and serious Design, all along, to do Honour to your Commission, and never to do the least Thing contrary to your Duty and Allegiance to the King: And this I have to say in your Defence, That several Persons at New York, who I can bring to evidence if there be Occasion, did tell me, That by several Advices from Madagascar and that Part of the World, they were informed of your Men's revolting from you in one Place; which I am pretty sure they said was at Madagascar; and that others of them compelled you, much against your Will, to take and rifle Two Ships. I have advised with his Majesty's Council and shewed them this Letter, this Afternoon; and they are of Opinion, That if your Case be so clear as you (or Mr Emmot for you) have said, then you may safely come hither, and be equipped and fitted out, to go and fetch the other Ship; I make no manner of doubt but to obtain the King's Pardon for you and those few Men you have left, who, I understand, have been faithful to you, and refused, as well as you, to dishonour the Commission you had from England.

I assure you, on my Word and Honour, I will perform nicely what I have now promised: Though this I declare beforehand, That whatever Treasure or Goods you bring hither, I will not meddle with the least Bit of them; but they shall be left with such Trusty Persons as the Council shall advise, until I receive Orders from England, how they shall be disposed of. Mr Campbell will satisfy you, That this that I have now writ is the Sense of the Council and of

Your humble Servant,

Bellomont

This letter of Bellomont has been severely criticized on the ground that he treacherously inveigled Kidd into surrendering himself by pledging his honour that Kidd would be pardoned. This is an unfair criticism; it is abundantly clear that Bellomont's promise was (quite naturally and properly)

conditional upon Kidd's ability to show that his protestations of innocence were justified. As will appear hereafter, Kidd was given every opportunity to vindicate himself, and it was not until his conduct clearly showed his guilt that he was arrested.

One other point is also of interest, in view of subsequent events. It will be noted that Kidd admitted the seizure of the two ships from which he took the French passes, and that he sent these passes to Bellomont. Now, if he believed that those passes justified him in seizing the two ships, why should he plead that the ships were seized violently by his men against his will? If they were French ships, it was his *duty* to seize them. It will be noted that at a later stage he abandons this story that the ships were seized against his will. Why, then, did he allege it now?

This letter was brought to Kidd by Duncan Campbell. During the latter's absence Kidd had transferred certain chests and goods from the *Antonio* into three sloops which had put out to Block Island. Why – if he were innocent?

Kidd then sent the following reply to Bellomont:

From Block Island Road, on Board the Sloop *St Antonio*.
June the 24th 1699

May it please your Excellency.

I am honoured with your Lordship's kind Letter of the 19th instant, by Mr Campbell; which came to my Hands this Day; for which I return my most hearty Thanks.

I cannot but blame myself for not writing to your Lordship before this Time, knowing it was my Duty; but the Clamours and false Stories that have been reported of me made me fearful of writing or coming into any Harbour till I could hear from your Lordship.

I note the contents of your Lordship's Letter: As to what Mr Emmot and Mr Campbell informed your Lordship of my Proceedings, I do affirm to be true; and a great deal more might be said of the abuses of my Men, and the Hardship I have undergone to preserve the Ship. And what goods my Men had left:

Ninety-five Men went away from me in one Day and went on board the *Moca Frigate*. Captain Robert Culliford, Commander; who went away to the Red Seas, and committed several Acts of Piracy, as I am informed, and afraid (the Men formerly belonging to my Galley) that the Report is gone home against me to the East India Company that I have been the Actor: A sheet of Paper will not contain what may be said of the Care I took to preserve the Owners Interest, and to come home to clear my own innocence. I do further declare the protest, That I never did in the least act contrary to the King's Commission, nor to the Reputation of my honourable Owners; and doubt not but I shall be able to make my Innocence appear; or else I had no need to come to these Parts of the World, if it were not for that, and my owners Interest. There are Five or Six Passengers that came from Madagascar to assist me in Bringing the Ship home, and about Ten of my own Men, that come with me, would not venture to go into Boston, till Mr Campbell had engaged, Body for Body, for them, That they should not be molested while I stayed at Boston, or till I return with the Ship. I doubt not but your Lordship will write to England in my favour, and for these few Men that are left. I wish your Lordship would persuade Mr Campbell to go home to England with your Lordship's Letters; Who will be able to give account of our Affairs, and diligently follow the same, that there may be a speedy Answer from England. I desired Mr Campbell to buy 1000 Weight of Rigging for fitting of the Ship to bring her to Boston, that I may not be delayed when I come there. Upon receiving of your Lordship's Letter, I am making the best of my way for Boston. This, with my humble Duty to your Lordship and Countess, is what offers from, my Lord,

Your Excellency's most humble and dutiful Servant,

Wm Kidd

This letter was duly carried to Boston by Duncan Campbell, who also brought to Lady Bellomont, as presents from Kidd, an enamelled gilt box with four diamonds set in gold, with two rings which were afterwards valued at sixty pounds. These were promptly handed over by Bellomont to the

Council. Kidd was, in fact, anxious to purchase the goodwill of everyone with whom he came in contact; to Duncan Campbell he gave a gold chain and some pieces of muslin; to the master of the sloop which conveyed Campbell out to the *Antonio* he gave a bale of white calico, some pieces of muslin, and some sugar; and to a companion of Campbell some pieces of Arabian gold. Kidd also promised five hundred pounds to Campbell if the latter could procure a pardon for him. At Block Island Mrs Kidd and children came on board. Kidd's next movements are noteworthy; instead of sailing straight for Boston, he made for Gardiner's Island, where he landed two bales of goods, a heavy chest (afterwards found to contain gold and silver), two or three other chests, two Negro boys, and a Negro girl – all of which were left in the care of Mr John Gardiner, a man of considerable substance and standing. Here also Kidd sold some bales of merchandise to the master of another sloop. Were these the actions of a man who was honestly anxious to take back to the promoters all the proceeds of the expedition? For some days Kidd was hovering between Gardiner's Island and Block Island, landing on each several times.

From Gardiner's Island Kidd made his way to Boston, putting in at Tarpolin Cove to land some bales of goods. On 30 June he exchanged courtesies with a Boston sloop and presented the master with a piece of a bar of gold, asking him also to take on board his sloop to Boston a bag containing pieces of eight, a Turkey carpet, a clock, a small bundle supposed to contain clothes belonging to Mrs Kidd, and a pair of stilliards. All these articles were accordingly transferred in to the Boston sloop.

On 2 July 1699, Kidd arrived off Boston and landed. He and his wife and children took up their quarters in a boarding-house kept by Duncan Campbell. Colonel Robert Livingston, greatly disturbed by the rumours which were current concerning the very man whom he had so strongly recommended for the command of the expedition, hastened to meet Kidd. Not satisfied, apparently, with Kidd's explanation's Livingston went to Bellomont and demanded to be released from the bond into which he had entered as Kidd's guarantor, but, as might be expected, he was not successful. Livingston was not, however, above accepting certain presents from Kidd.

On 3 July Kidd made his first appearance before Bellomont, who sat in Council in his house. Kidd's manner was truculent. He alleged that the journal of the voyage, which he had kept, had been destroyed by his mutinous men, and that he had not had time to prepare a full narrative to replace it. He was accordingly granted until five o'clock the next day to prepare and produce a detailed account of his movements and actions since leaving England. At the appointed time on 4 July Kidd again appeared before the Governor and Council, and again protested that the narrative was not yet ready. On this occasion he was accompanied by five of his crew. His attitude was still more truculent; he refused to disclose the exact spot where he had left the *Quedagh Merchant* in Hispaniola – indeed, he even denied that the ship he had left there was the *Quedagh Merchant*; and, despite the fact that his men had admitted that a Portuguese ship had been seized by the *Adventure Galley,* he denied this also. He was, nevertheless, allowed until 5 p.m. on the following day to produce a written narrative. On 5 July he again protested that he had not had time, and again the inquiry was accordingly adjourned for twenty-four hours. At the appointed time on 6 July Kidd did not appear; he was therefore sent for. He refused to come, saying that he had not yet finished the preparation of his written statement. Accordingly the Council resolved that he should be arrested – more particularly because rumours were current that he was intending to slip away to sea again.

Later in the day Kidd was arrested outside the door of Bellomont's house. He attempted to draw his sword, then broke away and rushed into the house, followed by the constable, who finally overpowered his prisoner in Bellomont's presence. In a search of Kidd's lodgings a quantity of gold dust and ingots was discovered between two feather beds.

Even with Kidd under arrest, Bellomont's mind was not at rest. He had found it no easy matter to persuade the Council to order the arrest. Public opinion was still in sympathy with the pirates, and at any moment might lead to an attempt to effect Kidd's release. Even the Provincial Assembly had rejected a Bill which Bellomont had recommended (on the instructions of the Home Government) for the punishment of pirates. So again Bellomont had recourse to the Council, who on 17 July resolved: 'That the said Captain Kidd be put into the Stone Prison, be Ironed, and Company kept from him.' It was feared that he might escape from the prison-keeper's house, in which he had hitherto been confined – a fear for which there was some justification, for, but a fortnight previously, a pirate named Bradish had escaped with the connivance of the gaoler.

Arrest had had a salutary effect upon Kidd. On 7 July Duncan Campbell was enabled to present to the Council a narrative of the voyage of the *Adventure Galley*, written in Kidd's own hand. Furthermore, Kidd disclosed the whereabouts of the *Quedagh Merchant*. Bellomont immediately gave orders for a ship to be fitted out to find her and bring her and the treasure back to Boston; but before the ship was ready to sail, one Captain Evertse, freshly arrived from Curaçao, brought the news that Boulton and his men had transferred the goods out of the *Quedagh Merchant* into a sloop, set her on fire, and sailed away from Hispaniola. There was also further evidence that her cargo had been sold by Boulton and his men in Curaçao. Bellomont had therefore to content himself with recovering such of the proceeds of the expedition as Kidd had disposed of in New England. Statements were taken from the men who had returned with Kidd – all of whom had been arrested, with the exception of four who escaped – and also from the skipper of the *Antonio*, and from all those who had any knowledge of Kidd's movements since arriving off the New England coast.

On instructions from the Admiralty, Kidd and his men were shipped as prisoners to London.

*

Kidd, as we have seen, was brought to London in the King's yacht. On 14 April he was privately examined before the Board of Admiralty – the Judge of the Admiralty Court being present – and was then sent to Newgate to be kept in irons. Nine days later, however, on his petition, his irons were knocked off.

We have seen that the House of Commons had insisted that Kidd should not be tried until the next session of Parliament. In view of the suspicions aroused by the connexion of the four powerful lords with the expedition, this attitude can hardly be deemed unreasonable, but it had one regrettable result, namely, that the prisoner was kept in Newgate awaiting trial for over a year. Kidd was arrested in Boston on 6 July 1699; he was not brought to trial at the Old Bailey until 8 May 1701! The modern conscience revolts at the thought of a man being kept in prison without trial for close on two years.

On 6 March 1701, Parliament having at last reassembled, the Commons ordered all papers in connexion with Kidd's expedition to be laid before them by the Admiralty. On the following day the documents were duly presented, but it was found that they were so mixed up with other documents relating to piracy that a special Committee was appointed to sort them. On 27 March Sir Humphrey Mackworth, the Chairman of the Committee, delivered the papers, duly sorted, at the clerk's table; the petition of one Cogi Babba (an Armenian, who was part-owner of the *Quedagh Merchant*), praying for justice in respect of his losses at Kidd's hands, was read, Cogi Babba appearing in person at the bar of the House; and Kidd was brought in from Newgate and examined.

It is evident that at this stage the Commons were desirous not so much for the punishment of Kidd as to obtain some evidence which would inculpate the four lords. It may reasonably be assumed that they hoped to obtain some such evidence from Kidd. Had they done so, they might well have been willing to obtain a pardon for him. But they were disappointed. Kidd made a poor showing; he was truculent, and obstinately denied all the accusations made against him; one account alleges that he was drunk. On hearing Kidd's answers, one member exclaimed: 'I had thought him only a knave. I now know him to be a fool as well.' On the following day Kidd was again examined, and Sir Edmund Harrison was sent for and examined also. The House then entered into debate, and a motion was put that the grant of pirates' goods should be declared illegal and therefore null and void; but the motion was defeated by 193 votes to 185 – a majority small enough to cause the four lords some consternation. The House then voted an Address to the King that Kidd be put on trial in the ordinary way, and on 1 April Mr Secretary Hodges announced that the King had ordered that this should be done.

Under date 16 April 1701 the following minute appears in the Journal of the House:

The House being informed that Captain Kidd had sent to the Commissioners for executing the office of Lord High Admiral of England, that he may have the use of his Commission, and some other papers, at his trial; which things now lie before the House.

53

Ordered, That the said Commission, and such other papers as Captain Kidd desires, be delivered, by the Clerk of this House, to the Secretary of the Admiralty.

Among these papers were the two French passes which Kidd had sent by Emmot to Bellomont, and which the latter had forwarded to the Admiralty. That these two French passes did exist there can be no doubt, for copies of them appear in the Journal of the House of Commons. Nevertheless, the passes were never allowed to reach Kidd's hands, and the judges at the trial were led by the prosecution to believe that no such passes existed. That this was grossly unjust cannot be denied; but as will be discussed later, it cannot fairly be said that it resulted in a miscarriage of justice.

On 8 May 1701, William Kidd appeared in the dock at the Old Bailey. There were six indictments against him, involving four separate trials. The first indictment charged him with the murder of William Moore, the gunner; the second indictment (second trial) with piracy in regard to the *Quedagh Merchant*; the third and fourth indictments (third trial), with piracy in regard to the ships seized by him on 20 September 1697 and 27 November 1697; the fifth and sixth indictments (fourth trial), with piracy in regard to the ships seized on 28 December 1697 and 20 January 1698. On the piracy charges there stood with him in the dock nine of his crew.

*

There were no less than six judges concerned in the trials of Kidd: Lord Chief Baron Ward, Baron Hatsell, Justices Turton, Gould, and Powell, and the Recorder of London, Sir Salathiel Lovell.

Sir Edward Ward (1638–1714) had acquired an extensive practice in the Court of Exchequer before being raised to the bench. In 1683 he had appeared as counsel for the ill-fated Lord William Russell, and, in another case, had gained notoriety by a heated passage of arms with Chief Justice Jeffreys. In 1689 he was appointed a judge of the Common Pleas, but four days later was excused at his own request. In 1693 he was appointed Attorney-General, and in 1695 raised to the bench as Lord Chief Baron of the Exchequer. Just previous to the Kidd trial Ward had sat as one of the judges in the Bankers' case, and was one of those who had declined to give an opinion. He was a careful and pains-taking judge, and his conduct during Kidd's trial for murder shows him to have been gifted with rare patience.

Sir Henry Hatsell, born in 1641, was called to the bar in 1667, took the coif in 1689, and was raised to the bench as Baron of the Exchequer in 1697. Mr Justice Turton, called to the bar in 1673, gained elevation by his support of the Revolution, being appointed Baron of the Exchequer in 1689, and was transferred to the King's Bench seven years later. Mr Justice Gould, called to the bar in 1667, serjeant in 1692, was made a judge of the King's Bench in 1699, and on his first circuit had the unusual experience of fining a baronet £100 for contempt of Court, the contempt con-sisting in kicking the High Sheriff and calling the Judge a liar.

Most picturesque of all is the figure of Mr Justice Powell (1645–1713). John Powell was called to the bar in 1671, sat as M.P. for Gloucester, and in 1691 was appointed Baron of the Exchequer, being transferred later to the Common Pleas. His reputation as a lawyer was of the highest, and as a man he was universally admired and liked. Dean Swift, in a letter to Stella, described Powell as 'an old fellow with grey hairs, who was the merriest old gentleman I ever saw, spoke pleasing things, and chuckled till he cried again'. Powell presided at the trial of Jane Wenham, who was accused of witchcraft. In the course of the trial it was alleged that she could fly, whereupon the judge smiled at the prisoner and remarked: 'You may – there is no law against flying.'

Of a different stamp was Sir Salathiel Lovell, Recorder of London, who opened the sessions at which Kidd was tried. He was old and incompetent. During his Recordership – to which he was elected by the casting vote of the Lord Mayor – he proved himself so forgetful that he was nicknamed the 'Obliviscor of London'.

The leader for the Crown at Kidd's trial was the Solicitor-General, Sir John Hawles, a man who had attained eminence at the bar very quickly, possibly through political influence, for he had sat as M.P. for Old Sarum, Wilton, St Michael, and Truro.

*

The allegation that Kidd did not have a fair trial has so often been made that it is well to examine it with some care.

In those days, it must be remembered, accused persons in criminal cases were obliged to conduct their own defence, and were not allowed counsel for the purposes of examining or cross-examining witnesses or of addressing the jury on questions of fact. Counsel were only permitted to appear on their behalf with the leave of the Court, and then solely for the purpose of addressing the bench on questions of law. On appearing in the dock, Kidd immediately applied that Dr Oldish and Mr Lemmon (who were present on his instructions) might be assigned to him as counsel. After much delay, caused by Kidd's obstinacy in refusing to plead, his application was granted, and his counsel then moved that the trial be postponed, on the ground that he had not yet been put in possession of the two French passes, which were among the papers that the House of Commons had ordered should be delivered to him.

The Court allowed the indictments for piracy to stand over until the following day, and Kidd was then put on his trial for murder. In regard to this trial, no remarkable complaint can be made; the jury found a verdict of guilty upon evidence which was not only clear, but was also strengthened by the questions put by Kidd in cross-examination, and sentence of death was duly passed.

The trials for piracy are, however, in a different category. Kidd was certainly placed at a grievous disadvantage. A prisoner in those days could not give evidence in his own defence; and since his men were charged with him in the same indictments, he was prevented from calling any of them as witnesses in his behalf. Undoubtedly, therefore, he was handicapped; but this was the necessary result of the rules of procedure of the day, and Kidd was prejudiced thereby no more than any other eighteenth-century prisoner. In his case, moreover, the handicap was theoretical rather than practical; for it is certain that the evidence of his co-prisoners (could they have been called) would have aided the prosecution rather than the defence; either they would have had to repeat the evidence given by them at their examination in Boston (which would have been fatal to Kidd), or, if they departed from that evidence they would have been confronted in cross-examination with the Boston depositions, with the inevitable effect upon the jury (which would have been equally fatal to Kidd).

The attacks made upon Kidd's trial are, however, based on other grounds: first, that he was wrongfully deprived of documents which, so it is suggested, would have provided him with a complete defence; secondly, that the evidence adduced by the prosecution was both insufficient and also so tainted – coming from former accomplices – that it was inadmissible without corroboration.

First, as to the withholding of documents. The documents referred to are, of course, the two French passes. It must be remembered that Kidd was charged with piracy in respect of five separate vessels; as regards three of these ships, it was never suggested that any French passes existed, and so the issue of those indictments was not, and could not be, affected by the non-production of the documents. But the indictments for the seizure of the *Quedagh Merchant* (second trial) and the *Maiden* (second indictment in the third trial) are in a different category. Here, indeed, there is grave cause for comment. It cannot be denied that a gross injustice was done to Kidd by the Admiralty in not handing those papers over to him or to his advisers, as ordered by the House; and a still greater injustice lay in the conduct of the prosecution in not admitting the existence of the two passes. Kidd kept cross-examining as to the existence of these; the witnesses for the prosecution replied (probably quite truthfully) that they had never seen them. And to make matters worse, this question of the existence of the passes was put to the jury (by Lord Chief Baron Ward in the second trial, and by Mr Justice Turton in the third trial) as a material question for their consideration. No blame can attach to either judge; each summed up with commendable fairness on the facts as before them; nevertheless, by the withholding of the passes from Kidd, the Admiralty prevented him from placing before the jury the true evidence on a question referred to them as a material one. To that extent, as regards these two indictments (but only as regards these two indictments), it may be conceded that Kidd did not have a fair trial.

But now we come to a different aspect of the problem, namely, did this highly regrettable feature in the case result in fact in a miscarriage of justice? It must be remembered that the passes could only have provided Kidd with a defence to the indictments if in fact the ships were (or were reasonably believed by Kidd to be) the property of French subjects or of persons domiciled in French dominions. It was not sufficient for Kidd merely to prove that he found a French pass on board each ship. And that is all he could have done, even if the passes had been produced. It is clear that in fact a French pass was produced by the Captain of each ship only because Kidd was flying French colours himself. If corroboration of this is needed, it is to be found in the statements procured by Bellomont from the very men who were standing beside Kidd in the dock. From the statement of William Jenkins, corroborated by Barlicorn and Lamley, it is manifest that other passes (besides the French passes) were produced, and that Kidd knew full well that both ships were Moorish ships, belonging to Moorish owners. Moreover, as Lord Chief Baron Ward pointed out more than once during the second trial, if these ships had been French ships which Kidd was entitled to seize, then Kidd was bound to have them condemned as prizes and had no right (as he did so) to share their cargoes with his men. A study of the evidence for the prosecution also clearly reveals that in fact the ships were Moorish, that the owners were Moors, and that Kidd knew it. For that reason, coupled with the additional point put by Lord Chief Baron Ward above, no reasonable jury could have failed to convict, even if the passes had been produced. So, although Kidd was unjustly treated by this wrongful suppression by the Admiralty of material evidence, yet it appears clear that that evidence (if produced) would not have affected the jury's verdict; and, especially in view of the further evidence of which we know, but which could not be placed before the jury at the trial, it is therefore clear that no actual miscarriage of justice resulted. Those who do not agree with this view may console themselves with the following thought: even had Kidd (by the production of the passes) been acquitted of the charges preferred in these two indictments – even then, he would still have suffered the extreme penalty in respect of the convictions on the indictment for murder and the three other indictments for piracy. But this does not obliterate the scar left upon the face of British justice.

Now, as regards the nature and cogency of the evidence for the prosecution. If the two witnesses called by the Crown

were to be believed, then their testimony was certainly
definite and comprehensive enough to justify a conviction.
And the jury did believe these witnesses. Those who quibble
at Kidd's conviction say that these witnesses should not have
been believed – or, alternatively, that their evidence was
not admissible without corroboration – because they were
accomplices. The two witnesses in question were Joseph
Palmer, who had served under Kidd in the *Adventure
Galley*, and Robert Bradinham, who had been the surgeon
on board that ship. These two men had left Kidd at
Madagascar, and had subsequently come home and been
pardoned under the proclamation issued by the Lords
Justices in November 1698. It is thus material to note that
these men had not turned King's evidence to save their own
skins; their pardon was not on account of, or conditional
upon, their appearance in the witness-box against Kidd;
they had already been pardoned before any question of
evidence arose. There was thus no inducement for them –
either of fear or reward – to give evidence which was not
true; indeed, in so far as they testified as to the piratic
exploits of the *Adventure Galley*, they could harm rather
than help themselves.

It will thus be seen that the usual reasons for regarding
the evidence of accomplices with suspicion were absent in
this case. Neither Palmer nor Bradinham stood to gain anything by his testimony. Those critics who allege that the
evidence of accomplices must be corroborated stretch even
the modern view of the law of evidence too far. As recently
as 1916 the Court of Criminal Appeal laid down the law
as follows:

The uncorroborated evidence of an accomplice is admissible in
law, but the jury should be warned of the danger of convicting
on such evidence. If, after such a warning, the jury convict, the
Court will not quash the conviction merely on the ground that
the evidence of the accomplice was uncorroborated, but it will

do so if it considers the verdict unreasonable or that it cannot be supported having regard to the evidence.

The obligation of pointing out to the jury the danger of convicting on such evidence had not been established in Kidd's day as a legal rule. Nevertheless, the jury were well aware of the character and past history of these two witnesses; and the jury believed them, as they were entitled to do. As one of the judges pointed out in reply to Kidd's protest, theirs was the only evidence that could be got in the circumstances. Moreover, the very nature of the questions put by Kidd in cross-examination only served to corroborate the testimony given against him.

Thus we may sum up. There were indeed features in the Kidd case which offend the modern conception of justice; he was kept in prison awaiting trial for nearly two years; he was deprived of the use of certain material papers at his trial, in defiance of the order of the House of Commons; he suffered, in common with all prisoners of the age, from the contemporary rules of procedure which forbade him or any of his co-prisoners to go into the witness-box in his defence, and which deprived him of the services of counsel for the purpose of cross-examination. Nevertheless, none of these grievances can be charged against his judges or the jury; within the limits prescribed by the rules of procedure of the day, Kidd was given a fair trial by both judges and jury – in fact, his judges exhibited great patience. Study of the evidence as a whole, and of the documents which were not (and could not be) placed before the Court, makes abundantly manifest the fact of Kidd's guilt and the substantial justice of his conviction.

*

For the final scenes of Kidd's life we are indebted to that prolix chronicler of criminals' last hours, the Rev. Paul Lorrain, Ordinary of Newgate.

The four trials occupied two days – 8 and 9 May. On 10 May Lorrain visited the convicted pirates and 'admonished them to self-examination and repentance'. The next day was Sunday; so Lorrain preached to them, choosing for his text the passage: 'And they shall go away into everlasting punishment.' From then on, in the approved manner of the day, Lorrain laboured daily, by the usual threats of eternal damnation and the promise of forgiveness to the repentant, to extract confessions from the condemned men. Kidd apparently remained adamant, 'vainly flattering himself with hopes of a reprieve'. To the very end he persisted in declaring his innocence. In Lorrain's own words:

I found him unwilling to confess the crime he was convicted of, or declare anything, otherwise than that he had been a great offender, and lived without any due consideration either of God's mercies or judgements or of His wonderful works which had often been set before him. That he never remembered to return Him thanks for the many great deliverancies he had received from Him nor called himself to account for what he had done. And now he owns that God is a just God and he a vile wretched sinner. He says he repents of his sins and hopes to be saved through the merits of Christ. He further declares that he dies in charity with all the world.

Now all this was highly unsatisfactory to the Rev. Paul Lorrain. He would sooner have had his inquisitive mind satisfied by a full and detailed confession in place of these pious sentiments. And he was a persistent man. So, on the day of the execution, he had Kidd in the chapel in the morning and again in the afternoon, and administered 'further admonitions of repentance', still without success:

I was afraid the hardness of Capt. Kidd's heart was still unmelted. I therefore applied myself with particular exhortations to him and laid the judgements of God against the impenitent and hardened sinners, as well as His tender mercies to those that were true and sincere penitents, very plain before him. To all of which he readily assented and said that he truly repented of his sins and forgave all the world, and I was in good hopes he did so. But having left him, to go a little before him to the place of execution, I found to my unspeakable grief, when he was brought thither, that he was inflamed with drink, which had so discomposed his mind, that it was now in a very ill frame and very unfit for the great work, now or never to be performed by him. [The 'great work' was presumably the confession which Lorrain was so anxious to obtain for publication.] I prayed for him and so did other worthy Divines that were present, to whom (as well as to myself) the Captain appeared to be much out of order, and not so concerned and affected as he ought to have been. 'Tis true he spake some words expressing his confidence in God's mercy thro' Christ, and likewise declared that he died in charity with the world, but still I suspected his sincerity, because he was more reflective upon others than upon himself, and still would endeavour to lay his faults upon his crew and others, going about to excuse and justify himself, much about the same manner as he did when upon his trial. When I left him at Newgate, he told me he would make a full confession at the tree, but instead of that (contrary to my expectation) he was unwilling to own the justice of his condemnation, or so much as the providence of God, who for his sins had deservedly brought him to this untimely end.

The gallows were at Execution Dock, overlooking the river at Wapping. This was the usual place of execution for pirates. It had a special significance for Kidd, for it was not far from here – only the other side of the water – that he had set out on his fatal voyage in the *Adventure Galley*. The date was the 23 May 1701.

All those who had been tried and convicted with Kidd had been reprieved, with the exception of Darby Mullins. Mullins was hanged first. Then came Kidd's turn. Having addressed the crowd, warning all masters of ships to take a lesson from his fate, he was turned off. But his end was not yet to come. The rope on which he was suspended broke. Kidd fell to the ground with the halter round his neck, and was found to be still alive and conscious. Yet this terrible incident had no horror for the Rev. Paul, who seized upon this further chance vouchsafed to him to extract a confession:

When he was brought up and tied again to the tree, I desired leave to go to him again, which was granted. Then I showed him the great mercy of God to him in giving him (unexpectedly) this further respite that so he might improve the few moments now so mercifully allotted to him in perfecting his faith and repentance. [The poor wretch was only half-conscious.] Now I found him in much better temper than before. But as I was unwilling, and the Station also very incommodious and improper for me, to offer anything to him by way of question that might perhaps have discomposed his Spirit, so I contented myself to press him to embrace (before it was too late) the mercy of God, now again offered to him, upon the easy conditions of steadfast faith, true repentance, and perfect charity. Which now he did so fully and freely express, that I hope he was hearty and sincere in it, declaring openly that he repented with all his heart, and died in Christian love and charity with all the world. This he said as he was on the top of the ladder (the scaffold being now broken down) and myself half-way on it, as close to him as I could, who, having again, for the last time, pray'd with him, left him, with a greater satisfaction than I had before that he was penitent.

At least Kidd could not be attacked upon the ground of want of courage. He had faced this last terrible ordeal unflinchingly.

*

One problem remains unsolved to this day. What became of the *Quedagh Merchant* and of the treasure that was supposed to be aboard her? Captain Evertse had reported that the ship had been burnt, and that Boulton and his men had seized everything she contained, selling the goods in Curaçao and other islands in the West Indies. At first this report was accepted, but as time passed rumours were circulated to the effect that Kidd's ship and treasure still lay hidden. From time to time, even so recently as during the last century, expeditions have been fitted out in search of it. Some declared that the ship had been sunk off the coast of Hispaniola, but the more popular view was that she had been brought to New England by Boulton, and sunk off the coast. The story that has obtained most credence is that she was brought up the North River, and scuttled and abandoned near the Highlands. The truth will presumably never be known.

The value of the goods and gold and jewels recovered from the sloop *Antonio* and from the various places where Kidd had hidden them in New England was £10,000. It was believed that the value of all that was left in the *Quedagh Merchant* was between forty and fifty thousand pounds.

Kidd's property and effects were forfeited to the Crown, and provided a sum of £6,471, which Queen Anne gave towards the establishment of Greenwich Hospital.

Dr Thomas Smethurst

· 1859 ·

BY

L. A. PARRY

THE trial of Dr Thomas Smethurst in 1859 for the murder of Miss Isabella Bankes by poison created at the time an exceptional amount of public attention. In the words of the Lord Chief Baron Pollock, who presided, 'the case was one of the most remarkable in all its circumstances that he ever remembered in his now long experience', and these words are fully justified by the extraordinary incidents surrounding it. The bigamous marriage, the immediate obscure illness of the new 'wife', the arrest of the doctor on a charge of attempted poisoning, his release on the same day on his own recognizances, the death on the next day of the lady, his rearrest, his trial for murder terminated by the serious illness of a juryman, his second trial, his conviction, the great public outcry, especially in the medical press, at the injustice of the verdict, the unprecedented action of the Home Secretary, Sir George Cornewall Lewis, in submitting all the facts to the well-known surgeon, Sir Benjamin Brodie, for an opinion as to the justice of the verdict, the reprieve and subsequent grant of a free pardon to Smethurst, his trial and conviction for bigamy, and, finally, his successful action in the Probate Court to prove the will of his alleged victim – all these features combine to make the case one of the most curious on record.

In 1859 Dr Smethurst was fifty-four years old, though he gave his age as six years younger, probably because he felt that he could then plead, as some excuse for his bigamy, that he was a callow youth entrapped into his first marriage by a woman very considerably older than himself. In appearance he was a man of small stature and insignificant mien, with a reddish brown moustache. He was a fully qualified medical practitioner, having obtained the diploma of a licentiate of the Society of Apothecaries about 1830, and later the degree of Doctor of Medicine of the University of Erlangen. He practised in London for nine years, and later went to Ramsgate, where he remained for three years. At some time he visited Grafenberg, where he studied Priessnitz's system of hydropathy, and on his return he wrote a work called *Hydrotherapia* and established a water-cure establishment at Moor Park, near Farnham, which later he sold to a Dr Lane. For the six years preceding his trial he had given up practice, and some part of this time he had devoted to travel on the Continent.

In 1828 he had married at St Mark's Church, Kennington, a Miss Mary Durham, who was twenty years his senior. (It was during this year that he was imprisoned for a while in Horsemonger Lane jail charged with obtaining goods by false pretences, but was discharged by the magistrate.) He and his wife appear to have been a fairly happy and contented couple, and in 1858 they were living together at a Bayswater boarding-house, where the doctor met a lady, Miss Isabella Bankes, possessed of considerable charms and some means. She was forty-two years old. It was not long before their acquaintance ripened so considerably that the landlady, disapproving of their behaviour, requested Miss Bankes to leave the house. Soon after this the doctor also made his departure and joined her. A wedding ceremony was performed at Battersea Church, and the couple settled down in Richmond.

Miss Bankes was until her marriage in reasonably good health, though subject to bilious attacks. Soon after, she was taken ill, and for the first few days her husband attended her. As she got no better it was decided to call in another doctor, and, on the advice of the landlady, Dr Julius, a well-known Richmond practitioner, was sent for. He first attended on 3 April, when he was told by Smethurst that his wife was suffering from violent diarrhoea and vomiting. He questioned her, and came to the conclusion that he had to deal with an ordinary case of diarrhoea, and ordered chalk mixture. Two days later she was much worse, and complained of a soreness of the mouth and of a burning sensation in the throat and abdomen. The vomiting was very frequent and very distressing. The diarrhoea continued, and, as the drugs tried led to no improvement, Dr Julius began to suspect that some irritant poison was being given to her. He asked his partner, Dr Bird, to see Miss Bankes. Various remedies were used by him without success, and he came to the same conclusion as his partner, but only after Dr Julius had mentioned his own fear to him. This is an important point on which contradictory statements were made, but in the witness-box Dr Bird was very definite and clear on the matter.

On 30 April – a Saturday – Dr Smethurst visited a Richmond solicitor, Mr Senior, taking with him a draft will in his own handwriting, and requested the lawyer to come the next day to execute it properly. This he did on Sunday, and Miss Bankes, described in the document as a spinster, left everything she possessed, with the exception of a brooch, to 'my sincere and beloved friend, Thomas Smethurst'.

As Miss Bankes did not improve, it was decided to call in Dr Todd, a well-known consultant attached to King's College Hospital. He agreed with the diagnosis of irritant poisoning, and had a stool examined, but no poison was found. Miss Bankes did not improve under Dr Todd's treatment. Another stool was examined, and arsenic was discovered in it. Upon this, Smethurst was taken into custody on a charge of attempted poisoning, but was at once released by the magistrates. Miss Bankes died the next day, and Smethurst was again arrested, this time charged with murder.

It was stated by one of Smethurst's landladies that during Miss Bankes's illness, up to the time of the arrest of the doctor, practically all food and medicine had been given to her by Smethurst himself, and he was invariably in the room when the other doctors paid their visits. On the few occasions when other people gave her food she did not vomit.

At the autopsy it was found that the deceased was five to seven weeks pregnant. In the stomach there was a large patch of effused blood, but no signs of ulceration or acute inflammation. There was some inflammation of the small intestine. The large bowel showed very extensive ulceration. No arsenic whatever was found in the body, but antimony in small quantities was discovered in the caecum, the small intestine, one of the kidneys (the other was for some reason not examined), and in some blood taken from the heart.

These, very briefly, are the facts which led up to the arrest of Dr Smethurst on the charge of poisoning Miss Bankes.

*

The trial took place at the Old Bailey in July 1859. It was interrupted on the second day by the illness of a juryman, and, as there seemed no prospect of his early recovery, was adjourned till the next sessions in August. The Lord Chief Baron Pollock was the judge on both occasions, having insisted on hearing the trial although it was not his turn on the roster. An objection on the grounds that he was a friend of Dr Taylor, one of the prosecution witnesses, was overruled. There appeared for the Crown, instructed by the Director of Public Prosecutions, Mr Serjeant Ballantine, Mr Bodkin, Mr J. Clerk, and Mr Mereweather. The prisoner was represented by Mr Serjeant Parry and Mr Giffard.

Mr Serjeant Ballantine, in his opening speech, outlined the history of the case as already described. He pointed out that he had to show first that the unfortunate lady died of poisoning, and, secondly, that the prisoner was the one who administered the poison. He contended that the accused had used his special knowledge of poisons to murder the deceased, and that he had done his best to shroud the whole affair in mystery. There never was any intention on the part of the prisoner that the union with Miss Bankes should be a permanent one, for when the prisoner was arrested there was found on him a letter written to his real wife, announcing his early return to her. Miss Bankes was possessed of property of her own to the value of some £1,700 or £1,800, and also a life interest in £5,000 which at her death passed to other members of her family. The prisoner had induced Miss Bankes to make a will leaving the money to him, and it was the obtaining of this money which was the motive for the murder.

Witnesses were first called to prove the circumstantial portion of the evidence. Mrs Smith, keeper of the Bayswater boarding-house, where Smethurst and Miss Bankes met, stated that she gave Miss Bankes notice to quit because of what she considered improper familiarity between her and the doctor. The deceased never had good health; she appeared to be delicate. When cross-examined, she said that Miss Bankes used to say she felt nausea when she took food, and that she was very bilious. She left the dinner table more than once because of sickness. Everyone in the house, including Miss Bankes, knew that Dr and Mrs Smethurst were man and wife. When Mrs Smethurst was ill the accused used to attend on her.

Mrs Robinson, the landlady of one of the houses where Smethurst and the deceased lodged in Richmond, said that Miss Bankes was taken ill towards the end of March. Dr Smethurst said he was not satisfied with her progress, so, on the recommendation of the witness, Mrs Robinson, Dr Julius was called in. The deceased and Smethurst appeared to be on particularly good terms. The accused supplied all that Miss Bankes took in the way of nourishment. Cross-examined, she said Dr Smethurst frequently went to London, and the doctors saw the patient when he was absent.

Mrs Robinson's daughter Elizabeth stated that vomiting took place just the same whether the accused was absent or with the deceased.

The medical evidence for the prosecution, which was of the very greatest importance, was given next.

Dr Julius stated that he attended Miss Bankes from 3 April till the day of her death, 3 May. Her symptoms were as follows: diarrhoea, vomiting, and burning pains in the mouth, throat, and stomach. None of the drugs taken did any good, and she became very much worse. Among the medicines he gave her were bismuth and grey powder. He became suspicious that some irritant poison was being administered to the patient, and he therefore asked his partner, Dr Bird, to see her. There was still no improvement. Her condition was so critical that Dr Todd, a well-known consulting physician, was called in. One of the evacuations of the deceased was examined by Dr Taylor, then Professor of Chemistry at Guy's Hospital, and as a result of his analysis an application was made to a magistrate, and Smethurst was arrested. He did not consider that the symptoms could be accounted for on any grounds other than that of irritant poisoning.

Mr Serjeant Parry, during his cross-examination of Dr Julius, asked him if he were a doctor of medicine.

Witness: Yes.
Mr Serjeant Parry: Is yours a London degree?
Witness: Yes.

Mr Serjeant Parry: What degree is it?

Witness: It is the Archbishop of Canterbury's degree.

Mr Serjeant Parry: What! Can he make a doctor of medicine?

The Lord Chief Baron: Yes; and he can also make a master of arts.

Mr Serjeant Parry: Did you take your degree as a matter of course?

Witness: Oh, dear, no! It is a very uncommon thing. I had to get a certificate from two members of the College of Physicians, stating that they had known me for a length of time, and that I was a proper person to have the degree.

Mr Serjeant Parry: And having that certificate you got the degree?

Witness: Yes; but it only entitles me to call myself 'doctor'.

The Lord Chief Baron: But you are a member of the College of Surgeons, and a member of the Society of Apothecaries?

Witness: Yes.

This power to grant medical degrees was a remnant of Papal authority, which was reserved to the Archbishop of Canterbury by a statute passed in 1533 in the reign of Henry VIII. The Medical Act, 1857, abolished any qualification to practise with these degrees unless they were granted prior to the passing of the Act.

The evidence of Dr Bird confirmed that of his partner, Dr Julius. He attributed the symptoms of the deceased to some irritant mineral poison given constantly in small doses, either arsenic or antimony. He did not believe Miss Bankes died of acute dysentery, and he knew of no form of natural disease to which her death could be attributed.

Mr Caudle, dispenser to the former two witnesses, said he prepared all the medicines sent to the deceased, and there was no arsenic or antimony in any of them. There were preparations of both these substances in the surgery, but all the poisons were kept in a locked cupboard.

Mr Barwell, assistant surgeon at the Charing Cross Hospital, gave evidence as to the making of an autopsy on Miss Bankes. The deceased was between five and seven weeks pregnant. The chief viscera were sent uncut to Dr Taylor, and they were examined by him and witness in conjunction. There was a large patch of effused blood at the cardiac end of the stomach, the rest of the mucous membrane was pale except near the pylorus. There was no ulceration. There was some inflammation at the commencement of the duodenum; the other parts of the intestine were slightly infected. In the lower three feet of the ileum the mucous membrane was very much thickened. That of the caecum was nearly destroyed by inflammation and ulceration: these appearances decreased along the colon and rectum. He could not reconcile them with any natural disease, but they were compatible with irritant poisoning.

Dr Wilks, of Guy's Hospital, said he was present at the post-mortem, and, excluding dysentery, he was not acquainted with any form of disease which would account for the appearances. The death of the deceased was most probably to be accounted for by some irritant.

Dr Todd said he was called in to see Miss Bankes, and went with Dr Julius. He inquired into the symptoms and the remedies used. He did not hear from Dr Julius that there was any suspicion of irritant poisoning. He did not actually examine the intestines, but, after hearing an account of the autopsy and of the symptoms, he believed the deceased died from irritant poisoning. He included within this term arsenic, antimony, and corrosive sublimate. He had never made a post-mortem on a person who had died from slow arsenic poisoning. Such cases were very rare. It was quite impossible that pregnancy alone could produce such intense ulceration of the bowels. The only natural disease which could account for the morbid appearances was acute dysentery.

Inspector M'Intyre said he apprehended the prisoner on a warrant on 2 May, charging him with feloniously administering poison to Miss Bankes, who was at that time alive. The prisoner was taken before a magistrate, and he said the poor lady might die in his absence; it was essential that he should be at home. He was released on his own recognizances. Witness went back to the house with Smethurst, and he took possession of some bottles, &c., which he gave to Dr Taylor. On hearing of the death of Miss Bankes the next day, he took Dr Smethurst into custody on a charge of wilful murder.

Mr Buzzard, who had been a staff surgeon during the Crimean War, and had seen a great many bowel complaints, said he had heard a description of the symptoms and of the findings at the autopsy; he knew of no form of dysentery or bowel complaint compatible with these. He should refer them to some irritant substance taken into the system.

Dr Babbington said he had seen several cases of acute dysentery. He had heard the symptoms and the post-mortem findings of the deceased described. He did not think she died of acute dysentery, but from the effects of irritant poisoning. He had had an extensive medical practice as an accoucheur, and had known cases of pregnancy in which violent vomiting, but not violent diarrhoea, was an urgent symptom in the first few weeks of pregnancy.

Dr Bowerbank said he had had twenty-three years' practice in Jamaica, where acute dysentery was common. The symptoms and appearances in this case were certainly not referable to this disease. Some of them might be traced to acute inflammation of the intestines. There was no natural disease to which he could attribute the symptoms. He thought they were those of irritant poisoning.

Dr Copland said he had seen many cases of dysentery in

Africa and on the Continent. Viewing the whole evidence, death could not be attributed to acute dysentery. In his opinion irritant poisoning was the cause. If it were due to arsenic, he would expect to find a certain amount of the poison in the body.

Dr Alfred Swaine Taylor, professor of chemistry at Guy's Hospital, stated that on 1 May he examined a bottle brought to him by Mr Buzzard. He used Reinsch's process, and obtained arsenic. On 5 May he had brought to him the stomach (unopened), the spleen, liver, gullet, uterus, and the large and small intestines, and on the 7 the kidneys and some blood from the heart, and, in addition, a number of bottles. He found no arsenic in any of these. He did find antimony in the small intestines, in the caecum, and in one of the kidneys. The other kidney was not examined. There was also some antimony in the blood from the heart, but none in any of the other organs. The total quantity of antimony did not exceed one-quarter to one-half grain. In a further bottle submitted to him he found arsenic, but later discovered that this was a mistake, due to impurity in the copper gauze which he had used for his test. He explained the absence of traces of arsenic in the kidneys by the administering of chlorate of potass, which would eliminate them. Considering all the circumstances, the symptoms described, and the findings at the autopsy, he could ascribe death to nothing but irritant poisoning.

During his cross-examination Dr Taylor acknowledged that, when before the magistrates and coroner, he had sworn that he had found arsenic in the bottle, and that he told the magistrate he had tested all his reagents first. He used the same copper gauze which he had employed for fourteen years. At the time he believed the arsenic he found in the bottle was placed there by someone else, and was not contained in his materials. He subsequently found he was wrong. As a general rule in slow arsenic poisoning he would expect to find arsenic in the tissues of the body.

Dr Odling, professor of chemistry at Guy's Hospital, gave evidence that he had assisted Dr Taylor in the examination, and agreed with his conclusions.

Professor Brand, professor of chemistry at the Royal Institution, said he examined some liquid from the bottle partly by Reinsch's test, partly by Marsh's. He found no arsenic. If he had made the test at the time Dr Taylor did, he would have come to the same conclusion as Dr Taylor, that arsenic was present; but before he made his test the chlorate of potass which was originally in the bottle had been removed, and it was this substance dissolving the copper, thus releasing the arsenic in the gauze, which had caused the mistake.

This concluded the medical evidence for the prosecution.

Mr Serjeant Parry, in his address on behalf of the prisoner, said he fully accepted the view of his learned friend that it was necessary to show first that Miss Bankes died of poisoning; secondly, that this poison was administered by Smethurst. He contended that neither of these two propositions had been proved. The next point that appeared to be relied upon was that the accused was represented to have kept the deceased entirely under his control, and that he never left her alone. This had been positively disproved. It was shown that he went several times to London, that he also went into the town, which was some way off, and that there were ample opportunities for the deceased to communicate with any one she wished to. He should contend with great confidence that there was no evidence that the accused practised any concealment, either with reference to the disease from which the dead lady had been suffering, or any other matter.

Next, there was the question of the will. He believed that the will which had been made by the deceased was the entire foundation for the charge, and that none would have been made against the accused if this will had not been executed. It might be said that this supplied the motive; but, if the other evidence was insufficient to support the charge that the accused had wilfully destroyed the life of this lady, it appeared to him that the existence of the will ought not to be allowed to operate in any way upon their judgement. Supposing that the will were taken as evidence of a motive, what was the allegation? It was that Dr Smethurst had perpetrated this crime to obtain possession of some £1,800; but he would equally have come into possession of it if the deceased had lived, for it was clear that she was deeply attached to him, and that she had handed over to him the dividend she had received in April. While she lived she was also entitled to a life interest in £5,000, and the accused would have had the benefit of that in addition. He therefore had a much stronger motive for keeping her alive than he had for destroying her. Again, could there be any doubt that the will was the act of the deceased as much as it was of the accused, just as much as the marriage was her act as much as it was his?

He now came to the evidence of poisoning. It was said that death arose from the administration of some irritant poison such as arsenic or antimony. In the first place, had any arsenic or antimony or any other poison been shown to have been either directly or indirectly in the possession of the accused; had he had anything to do with any poison or had any poison within his reach or under his control? As for the stupid theory that the poison had been eliminated by the taking of chlorate of potass, it would be exploded long before the conclusion of the trial, if it were not already. It was merely the offspring of a fertile brain to account for what was felt to be an almost overwhelming difficulty in the way of the prosecution, namely, the absence of any poison in the body of the deceased. He would ask the jury whether they had ever heard of a conviction for murder by poison without some evidence being adduced that the accused had poison in his possession or that he was in a position to obtain it. It was said that he had an opportunity of making away with the poison if he were so minded; but this was not the fact, for he was taken suddenly into custody; he was searched, and he had no opportunity of concealing the poison, if there had ever been any in his possession.

The learned Serjeant then referred to the evidence of Dr Taylor, and reminded the jury that, when he was originally examined, he stated, distinctly and positively and without reservation, that he had discovered arsenic in a vessel that was in the control of the accused. If this had been a fact it would have been almost conclusive evidence against the accused, and if the mistake had never been found out, upon that fact alone the accused would have gone to the scaffold. Would they not pause before they gave effect to the medical testimony after this extraordinary error? Dr Taylor believed he was right, but he was wrong. What reliance ought to be placed on evidence of this description when the life of a fellow-creature was at stake? The same test was applied to the evacuation as was applied to the bottle referred to, and how were they to believe that a mistake had not been made with this as with the other? He would prove that in common grey powder there was frequently found antimony, and in bismuth there was often found arsenic. They would remember that Dr Taylor admitted that in the sulphate of copper which had come from the surgery of Dr Julius he had found slight traces of arsenic. He should be able to show them that not only had the deceased lady not died of poison, but that she had died of a natural disease.

The address of Serjeant Parry somehow carried little conviction.

A juryman, in a letter to *The Times* just after the trial, wrote as follows:

Sir, – In order to remove any impression that may exist in the minds of the public in respect to the summing-up of the judge having a tendency to influence the minds of the jury, I beg to inform you that at the close of the defence, and before the judge commenced his summing up, eleven of the jury were convinced, upon the evidence adduced, of the prisoner's guilt, and the remarks of the judge confirmed their opinions. – I am, sir, yours,

One of the Jury

It is extraordinary that, with such remarkable opportunities, the learned Serjeant was not able to make better use of material for the defence, and to impress the judge and jury to a greater degree.

A barrister, Mr L. H. Gent, of the Temple, made the following comments at the time of the trial: 'As a barrister belonging to and attending the bar at the sittings of the Central Criminal Court, I have gained, I believe, some little experience in criminal trials. I was present during a greater part of Smethurst's trial . . . and I heard no one but myself during its progress pronounce any decided opinion. My declaration throughout was that the trial was a "sham", a "mockery"; in my whole experience I never witnessed, nor I dare say ever shall witness, anything so extraordinary. Spectators, witnesses, prisoner's counsel, judge, jury, prosecuting counsel, one and all seemed weighed down, absolutely unable to escape from some mysterious weight hanging over their imaginations, which impelled them to a belief in the prisoner's guilt. Even the prisoner's counsel put his questions as though this evil influence led him every time to expect an unfavourable answer, and he got it. How I longed for some men whom I have known at the bar to rush in and break this solemn spell.'

This whole atmosphere was created, I believe, by the terrible preliminary mistake made by Dr Taylor, a mistake which grossly prejudiced the position of the prisoner, and nearly cost him his life.

The only evidence called for the prisoner was of a medical and chemical nature.

Dr B. W. Richardson stated that he was a doctor of medicine and professor of physiology at the Grosvenor Place School of Medicine. In his opinion the symptoms of the deceased were not reconcilable with slow arsenical poisoning. There was an absence of several symptoms he should expect to find. The results of the post-mortem examination also were against a case of poisoning of this description, as the inflammation was most developed in that part of the intestines which in arsenical poisoning generally received the least injury. He should expect arsenic to be found in the tissues of the body, especially the liver. The same applied to antimony. The symptoms of the deceased more resembled acute dysentery than slow arsenical or antimony poisoning. He had seen patients suffering from diarrhoea and vomiting with severe abdominal pain in pregnancy, and believed that this would account for all the symptoms of the deceased. He had analysed many samples of bismuth and found arsenic in them, as much as half a grain to the ounce.

Mr Rodgers said he had been a lecturer on chemistry at St George's School of Medicine. If arsenic and antimony had been administered to anybody for five or six weeks, he should certainly expect to find them in the tissues of the body, especially in the liver, kidneys, and spleen. If he did not find any poison, he should form the opinion that none had been administered. He could state positively that nearly all bismuth that was sold contained arsenic, and that grey powder contained antimony. The condition of the intestines of the deceased was not consistent with slow arsenical poisoning. If he did not find any poison in the body, he should doubt whether the experiment on the evacuation was a correct one. It was possible to obtain perfectly pure copper, and it was a most dangerous thing to use copper of any other description, especially if a man's life were at stake.

Dr Thudicum, lecturer on chemistry, said he had heard the evidence of the symptoms and of the post-mortem appearances, and all these were consistent with death from natural causes. In his opinion, Miss Bankes died of dysentery. The symptoms were not those of slow arsenic or antimony poisoning. If death had been due to poison, it should have been found in the tissues of the body. He had analysed grey powder and bismuth, and had found they both contained arsenic and antimony. He thought that these substances detected by Dr Taylor might be accounted for by the impurities in the grey powder and bismuth taken by the deceased.

Dr Webb, lecturer on medical jurisprudence at the Grosvenor Place School of Medicine, and physician to the Great Northern Hospital, said he thought the deceased died a natural death. He also expressed the opinion that the pregnancy of the dead woman was a material factor in the case, and that it would account for many of the symptoms. He was examined at very great length on post-mortem appearances, and he stated that these justified him in his opinion that death was due to natural causes and not to poison.

Dr Girdwood said that he had had a considerable experience in midwifery, and had seen many cases in which pregnancy was combined with dysentery. He thought this was the most probable cause of death in this case.

Mr J. Edmonds, medical officer to the H Division of the Police, said that in the early stages of pregnancy there is frequently severe diarrhoea and vomiting. He had had a fatal case. In it there was very severe ulceration of the caecum and lower bowel.

Dr Tyler Smith said pregnant women were liable to dysentery. Heartburn was also a common disorder in this condition. Menstruation was not an uncommon condition in the first two or three months of pregnancy. In some of the cases of vomiting in pregnancy he had seen the stomach retain food a few days before death.

Serjeant Ballantine, in his closing speech for the prosecution, dealt with the evidence of the various witnesses. He was not prepared to say positively that death was due either to arsenic or antimony, but it was due to some poison or other, when and where administered he was unable to say. He contended that the evidence of those who had attended the deceased throughout her illness was of more value than those who had appeared for the defence and had never seen her.

The Lord Chief Baron Pollock, in his charge to the jury, went very fully into all the evidence given in the case, occupying some nine hours in his address. He pointed out that the first thing they had to determine was whether the deceased had met her death by poison or not. If so, had the poison been administered by the prisoner? The learned counsel for the accused had endeavoured to show there was no pecuniary motive for the death of the deceased, inasmuch as during her lifetime the prisoner would enjoy her income of some £220, most of which would disappear at her death. But, on the other hand, it must be remembered that he would come into the immediate possession of about £1,800. It was a fact in favour of the accused that neither arsenic nor antimony had been found in his lodgings or in his possession when arrested. But at this time it was clear that the case was hastening to its end, so that, if poison were the cause of death, no more of the deadly ingredient was required. It must be remembered, too, that just before the death he was in the house all night by himself, so that the fact that no poison was found was not of so much importance.

He commented on the mistake made by Dr Taylor, but could not regard this as sufficient reason for the advice of

Serjeant Parry to disregard altogether the evidence of that doctor.

Dealing with the evidence given for the accused by the doctors, he said it appeared to be to the effect that, according to their opinion and experience, the symptoms that had been deposed to were not consistent with a case of slow arsenical poisoning, and that a great many symptoms that were almost invariably exhibited in such cases were absent in this lady.

Something had been said respecting several of the witnesses coming from a particular institution, and of their having been examined at the trial of Palmer, the poisoner, but it appeared to him that neither of these facts was of the slightest importance, and that their testimony ought to be considered irrespective of either of these circumstances.

The learned judge made these remarks because, at the trial, capital had been made of the fact that several of the witnesses for the defence were connected with the Grosvenor School of Medicine, one of the private medical schools of London, a species of institution which flourished in the first half of the nineteenth century before the hospital schools were properly organized. They have long since ceased to exist. The Grosvenor Place School was established in 1830, close to St George's Hospital, and closed in 1863. Many well-known medical men were attached to it, including Dr (afterwards Sir) Spenser Wells. It was sought to prejudice the testimony of these witnesses, as, being friends and colleagues, they might be inclined to agree in their evidence. It was also hinted that some of them had given evidence recently in favour of Palmer, the Rugeley poisoner, and that they might therefore be looked upon as habitually appearing in favour of accused persons.

The learned judge, continuing his remarks, said that another portion of the evidence went to show that the deceased might have died of some natural disease, but none of the witnesses went so far as to state that she actually did die of such disease. Those witnesses also expressed their opinion to be that in the case of death from either arsenic or antimony some portion of these substances would be found in the body, and particularly in the liver of the deceased.

He did not agree with the counsel for the accused that the real question was for the jury to consider which set of medical witnesses were entitled to credit. The medical evidence was, of course, very important, but the jury must, in addition, look at all the other facts of the case, and particularly at the conduct of the accused and his motives for committing the crime. They must, after all, be guided by those rules of common sense that would operate on the minds of reasonable men with regard to the more important actions of their lives, and even supposing that there was no medical testimony at all in the case, they would still have a very grave question to decide with reference to the guilt or innocence of the accused.

The jury were forty minutes deliberating, and then returned a verdict of guilty. The judge, before passing sentence of death, said he thought it would have been impossible to come to any other conclusion. Thus ended this very remarkable trial.

*

After sentence of death had been passed, the warrant of the Court, signed by the Lord Chief Baron, was handed to Mr Jonas, the Governor of Newgate, for the removal of the condemned man to the county jail of Surrey at Horsemonger Lane. A great crowd had collected to see the prisoner, but the chief warders took him out by a back way, and he was safely in jail before it was known he had left Newgate.

For a great many years Monday was the day upon which

executions took place in the county of Surrey, but, as this meant the erection of the scaffold on the top of the jail on Sunday, adverse criticism led to the alteration of the day to Tuesday, and, according to the custom of the time, Tuesday fortnight was fixed for the carrying out of Smethurst's sentence.

From the moment sentence was passed doubts were entertained whether it would be carried out. It was said that during the trial an opinion was expressed in a high quarter that it was a case for a conviction, but not one in which the death penalty should be insisted on. This feeling was strengthened by the fact that the Lord Chief Baron, in passing sentence, omitted to tell the prisoner that there was no hope, and he should prepare to leave this world. This was always done in cases where the judge intended to advise against any commutation of the sentence.

Probably in no case of which we have any record has such a controversy taken place on the result of a trial prior to the controversy over the recent Evans and Christie trials. The verdict was received by the public with mixed feelings, but by far the greater number, if we can judge from the correspondence in the Press, protested against it. A large and important section of the public, including many well-informed medical men, expressed very grave doubts as to the guilt of Dr Smethurst, or, perhaps, in many cases, as to whether his guilt had been brought home to him. There were so many elements of uncertainty in the chain of evidence that many of those, who in their heart accepted the verdict as just, felt that the guilt of the prisoner had not been legally proved.

The *Lancet*, one of the leading medical journals of the day, voiced the feelings of this section of the public in a strongly worded article, pointing out that the main question was whether the medical and chemical evidence was sufficient to prove that Smethurst had committed murder.

The Times, in a leader published just after the trial, contended that the doubt and suspicion attaching to Smethurst were so great that no one would venture to pronounce him innocent. But at the same time the mistakes and contradictions in the chemical evidence, the failure to detect pregnancy during life, and the possibility that the death of Miss Bankes might have arisen from natural causes, all concurred to render the certainty of the guilt of the condemned man anything but unequivocal. Doubt of so serious a character was attached to the case that the execution of Smethurst on the present conviction was an impossibility. No Secretary of State would undertake the terrible responsibility of such an act.

Another important medical paper, the *Medical Times and Gazette*, thus summed up its views:

Is the prisoner guilty? – We believe he is.
Was he *proved* guilty? – Certainly not.
The balance of probabilities was against him, but there is a *possibility* that he may be innocent. Innocent men have been hanged upon circumstantial evidence as strong as that which led to Smethurst's sentence. The very possibility of such a judicial murder is so dreadful that, while retaining the conviction of the guilt of the prisoner, forced on us by a consideration of the whole circumstances of the case, and without a particle of sympathy for him personally, we should gladly strengthen by any means in our power the petition to the Government not to carry out the irrevocable sentence of death.

The *British Medical Journal* took exactly the same attitude on the question. It was under no illusion as to the character of Smethurst. It referred to him as a man with whom no decent person could feel the least sympathy – a liar, a cheat, a scoundrel of the blackest dye in every walk of life. But as the following quotations from the leading articles on the matter will show, no doubt was felt that the charge of murder had not been satisfactorily proved:

Whether the verdict pronounced against him be a just one or not, the Great Judge alone can show. The doubt in the public mind on this point is so great that no one has a right to speak dogmatically; but we do not think we err in stating that, as far as the medical evidence goes, the profession have made up their minds that it is not sufficient to prove the charge against him. If it can be shown, as we think it reasonably can, that natural causes may have brought about a similar train of symptoms to those which the unfortunate Isabella Bankes suffered, and if it can be proved that death from such causes is far from an extraordinary circumstance, we think the medical public have a right to demand that the proofs of poisoning be so clear that no reasonable man can have a doubt about the matter.

Yet how do we find that the case really stands? Of the medical witnesses examined upon the trial, ten were of opinion that the woman was poisoned, and seven that her death might be accounted for by natural causes. Here, at least, is a division of opinion in the skilled evidence which should make us pause. Was it an irritant poison, or an irritable uterus, or the ulcerated bowel of dysentery which did the poor lady to death? We confess that, as far as we can judge, her pregnant condition was quite sufficient to account for the symptoms under which she laboured. There is one very remarkable circumstance which has not, we believe, been noticed, namely, that the commencement of the fatal illness of Isabella Bankes tallies very exactly with the commencement of her pregnancy. . . . It may be urged, however, that the mere simulation of symptoms of poisoning, which arise in some cases of pregnancy, affords no proof whatever that this was not a genuine case of poison. Here toxicology comes in to complete the inquiry. In nearly every case of poisoning of late years one of two things has been clearly proved – either poison has been found in unmistakable quantities in the body, or it has been traced to the possession of the supposed murderer. . . . In the present case, however, no poison whatever was traced to the prisoner; no arsenic whatever was found in the viscera of the deceased; and but a very small proportion – less than a quarter of a grain – in four ounces of evacuated matter; a trace of antimony was also found in the large intestines. In dealing with such minute quantities, if they are to be considered to weigh down the life of a human being, we ought to be very certain that no possible source of error could arise in the method of their detection. We are very far from having reduced chemistry to an exact science. This trial, indeed, proves how far. Dr Taylor swore before the magistrates at Richmond that he found arsenic in a bottle of solution of chlorate of potass in the possession of the prisoner; and it was inferred that the action of the last-named drug upon the kidneys tended to eliminate the poison from the system, thus accounting for its absence from the tissues of the body. Had Smethurst been tried on this evidence directly after his committal by the Richmond magistrates, his life would have fallen through this illusive gauze wire, and Dr Taylor might possibly, when too late, have discovered his lamentable error. This fact should, we think, act as a terrible warning to him; and we hope that he will not persist, as he said he should, in using the impure copper gauze in future experiments where human life is at stake. . . . If . . . the man who holds in his hands the keys of life and death will not insist upon purity in his tests, then we say that the horrors which flourished in the days of witch-craft, when human life hung upon the lips of any old crone, will be but too faithfully represented by the horrors which will flow from the pseudo-scientific evidence of the present day. . . . The judge, indeed, seemed to think that it was of no possible consequence to the jury to dwell upon the scientific evidence. For instance, when the foreman of the jury fainted at the details of the post-mortem examination, the judge said, 'it appeared to him that it was quite unnecessary to go into these matters with such minuteness, particularly as the jury would understand very little of the matter.' A more extraordinary statement than this never emanated from the judgement seat. Why, the post-mortem appearances of the intestine were of the utmost importance in enabling the jury to come to a proper conclusion as to whether death arose from poisoning or any other cause. It may be all very well for jurymen to faint under such an ordeal; but the judge should have at least remembered that the life of a human being was at stake, to whom these appearances were of the most vital importance. The conduct of the judge, however, in various parts of the trial, and especially in the summing up, was rather that of an advocate for the prosecution than of the occupant of the bench holding fairly the trembling balance of justice.

Two more extracts are given, the first from the *Dublin Medical Press*, the second from the *British Medical Journal*, to show the heated personalities indulged in, as a result of the remarkable differences of opinion in the medical evidence.

From the *Dublin Medical Press*:

So much for the position to which the members of the medical profession, in their capacity as witnesses in criminal trials, have been degraded by Drs Todd, Taylor, Julius, Bird, and Co. They have not left behind them one fixed opinion to guide the public press. The man who, *par excellence*, was looked upon as the pillar of medical jurisprudence; the man who it was believed could clear up the most obscure case, involving medico-legal considerations, ever brought into a Court of justice; the man without whose assistance no criminal suspected of poisoning could be found guilty in England; the man whose opinion was quoted as the highest of all authorities at every trial where analysis is required, is the same who has now admitted the use of impure copper in an arsenic test where a life hung upon his evidence, the same who has brought an amount of disrepute upon his branch of the profession that years will not remove, the ultimate effects of which it is impossible to calculate, which none can regret with a deeper feeling of sorrow than ourselves, though, perhaps, in the end, a lesson may be taught which will not be lost upon the medical jurists, and which may tend to keep the fountain of justice clear and unpolluted. We must look now upon Professor Taylor as having ended his career, and hope he will immediately withdraw into the obscurity of private life, not forgetting to carry with him his favourite arsenical copper. He can never again be listened to in a Court of justice, and should henceforth leave the witness-box to the occupation of others.

From the *British Medical Journal*:

The farce must no longer be exhibited to the world of the three most celebrated toxicologists of the country contradicting each other in matters where there should be no possibility of doubt. Dr Taylor, throughout his ample volume on poisons, never allows an opportunity to escape of sneering at the scientific attainments of Mr Herepath; and the latter gentleman, we must confess, is not behindhand in returning the compliment. Dr Letheby is equally complimentary to Dr Taylor. A sort of triangular duel goes on between these three toxicologists, whenever occasion arises. The public at large are scandalized, and ask in amazement, whether there can be anything in poison-hunting which breeds these unnatural storms in regions where the calm atmosphere of science should alone prevail. The public should no longer have exhibited to them the spectacle of professional men stabbing each other's reputation over the bodies of malefactors; and the medical profession, if it is wise, will strain every nerve to put an end to such suicidal proceedings.

In all papers, both medical and lay, heated controversies took place on the case. Individuals and combinations of individuals bombarded the Home Secretary, Sir George Cornewall Lewis, with letters, petitions, and suggestions. Thirty medical men practising in London, headed by Richard Quain, petitioned Sir George to exercise the Royal prerogative of mercy on the ground that there was nothing to justify the verdict of guilty; twenty-nine barristers, headed by Mr H. Tindal Atkinson, sent in another memorial asking that the sentence should not be executed, because they did not consider the evidence warranted the verdict; and the wife of Smethurst was among those who begged for the remission of the sentence.

The Home Secretary forwarded all these various documents to the judge who had conducted the trial, and the Lord Chief Baron, after full consideration, made the following report:

The medical communications which have since reached you put the matter in a very different light, and tend very strongly to show that the medical part of the inquiry did not go to the jury in so favourable a way as it might, and indeed ought to have done, and in two respects – (1) That more weight was due to the pregnant condition of Miss Bankes (a fact admitting, after the post-mortem, of no doubt) than was ascribed to it by the medical witnesses for the prosecution; (2) that, in the opinion of a considerable number of medical men of eminence and experience, the symptoms of the post-mortem appearances were ambiguous, and might be referred either to natural causes or poison. Many also have gone so far as to say that the symptoms and appearances were inconsistent and incompatible with poison.

On the other hand, the Chief Baron made reference to disclosures made since the trial, which in his opinion confirmed the guilt of the prisoner. The report concluded as follows:

I think there is no communication before you in all or any of the papers I have seen upon which you can rely or act. That from Dr Baly and Dr Jenner seemed to me to be the most trustworthy and respectable; but there is an unaccountable but undoubted mistake in it which must be rectified before it can be taken as the basis of any decision. If you have been favourably impressed by any of the documents, so as to entertain the proposition of granting a pardon or of commuting the sentence to a short period of penal servitude, I think it ought to be founded on the judgement of medical or scientific persons selected by yourself for the purpose of considering the effects of the symptoms and appearances and the result of the analysis, and I think, for the prisoner's sake, you ought to have the points arising out of Herepath's letter further inquired into and considered. I forbear to speculate upon facts not ascertained; but if Dr Taylor had been cross-examined to this, and had given no satisfactory explanations, the result might have been quite different.

The allusion to the mistake in the letter of Dr Baly and Dr Jenner is as follows:

We would further remark with regard to the symptoms present that Dr Julius appears to have been in attendance on Isabella

Bankes before he heard of vomiting as a symptom; this absence
of vomiting at the commencement is quite inconsistent with the
belief that an irritant poison was the original cause of the disease.

If this had been an accurate statement of fact, it would
undoubtedly have been an important point in Smethurst's
favour, but actually Dr Julius in his evidence very definitely
stated that vomiting was present from the commencement
of his attendance.

The reference to 'points arising out of Herepath's letter'
was this: Mr Herepath had published in *The Times* a
letter in which he asserted that Dr Taylor had extracted
from the bottle more arsenic than could have been contained in the amount of copper gauze used, thus implying
that Dr Taylor was an incompetent analyst. If this statement of Mr Herepath were a fact, it would have shown how
faulty was the analysis, for it was clearly proved that whatever arsenic was found in the bottle was contained in the
gauze, and in that only.

The Home Secretary, after considering this report of the
Lord Chief Baron, took a most unprecedented course. He
referred the whole matter, from the medical point of view,
to Sir Benjamin Collins Brodie, at that time the best-known
surgeon in London, having succeeded to this position on the
retirement of Sir Astley Cooper. He was on the surgical
staff of St George's Hospital, and was Serjeant Surgeon
to Queen Victoria, having previously held that post to
George IV and King William. After receiving Sir Benjamin's report, the Home Secretary addressed the following letter to the Lord Chief Baron, at the same time sending
a copy to *The Times*:

Whitehall, 15 November 1859

My lord – I have the honour to acknowledge receipt of your
lordship's further report, of the 18th ult., on the case of Thomas
Smethurst, who was convicted at the Central Criminal Court in
August last of murder, and sentenced to death.

As your lordship suggests in that report, that reference should be made to the judgement of medical and scientific persons selected by the Secretary of State, for the purpose of considering the symptoms and appearances of the deceased Isabella Bankes, and the result of the analysis, I have sent the evidence, your lordship's reports, and all the papers bearing upon the medical points of the case, to Sir Benjamin Brodie, from whom I have received a letter, of which I enclose you a copy, and who is of opinion that, although the facts are full of suspicion against Smethurst, there is not absolute and complete evidence of his guilt.

After a very careful and anxious consideration of all the facts, I have come to the conclusion that there is sufficient doubt of the prisoner's guilt to render it my duty to advise the grant to him of a free pardon, which will be restricted to the particular offence of which he stands convicted; it is my intention to institute a prosecution against him for bigamy.

The necessity which I have felt for advising Her Majesty to grant a free pardon in this case has not, as it appears to me, arisen from any defect in the constitution or proceedings of our criminal tribunals. It has arisen from the imperfection of medical science, and from the fallibility of judgement, in an obscure malady, even of skilful and experienced medical practitioners. – I have, &c., G. C. Lewis.

This last paragraph caused great offence to the medical fraternity, who regarded it as an uncalled-for slight on their profession. Considering the medical evidence given at this trial, so absolutely and uncompromisingly contradictory, it is hardly to be wondered at that a layman should have doubts as to the value of scientific testimony, if that were a sample.

*

Over a hundred years have passed since this trial took place. Is it possible, after this long interval of time, to throw any further light on it, to clear up any of the obscure points? It is interesting to examine the facts and to speculate on the question of the guilt or innocence of Smethurst. Did the circumstantial evidence of the witnesses at the trial prove the case for the prosecution? Did Dr Smethurst refuse to allow Miss Bankes to see her doctors alone? It was admitted by the prosecution's own witness that the prisoner frequently went to London or into the town of Richmond, and that during that time the doctors did visit Miss Bankes. Did Miss Bankes know that Dr Smethurst was a married man? There can scarcely be any doubt about this. He was living with his wife in Bayswater, in the same house as Miss Bankes, and everybody knew them as man and wife. It is, of course, just possible that Smethurst may have persuaded Miss Bankes that he was not really married to the lady, but just living with her. But against this is the fact that when the deceased made her will, after the marriage ceremony with the prisoner, she signed herself Isabella Bankes, spinster.

The witnesses for the Crown proved in cross-examination that Miss Bankes was 'of a bilious nature' and had a tendency to vomiting; that her illness coincided with the commencement of her pregnancy; that it was not so very strange that Smethurst himself should nurse her – he had done it for Mrs Smethurst when she was ill; that it was Dr Smethurst himself who, soon after the deceased was taken ill, asked for another doctor to be called in; that whether the prisoner were present or absent in London the vomiting took place just the same.

The question of motive is of considerable importance. What reason could Dr Smethurst have had for murdering Miss Bankes? Fear and cupidity are the only possible suggestions – fear of punishment for bigamy, possibly fear of the birth of a child, and the subsequent responsibility which would be cast on him; and cupidity, the immediate possession of a capital sum of about £1,800, which he could use as he wished. These reasons seem totally inadequate for the commission of the cold-blooded and brutal murder of a woman, whom he had treated as his wife, and to whom he appeared to be devoted, especially when it is remembered that the risk of prosecution for bigamy could not have been very great, for his real wife was obviously a consenting party, or at least was quite complacent about the matter; and also when one recalls the fact that the financial aspect of the death was on the whole to the disadvantage of Smethurst rather than to his advantage, for, though he would get the £1,800 at once, he would lose the interest in £5,000, which went at the death of Miss Bankes to her relatives. There was also the possibility, though a remote one, of Miss Bankes inheriting a further £35,000.

In connexion with the likelihood of the birth of a child, the following consideration is worth mentioning. Is it a possibility that instead of a mineral irritant being used, one of the many vegetable irritants, e.g., elaterium, colchicum, savin, veratrine, or croton oil, all of which are employed for the purpose of procuring abortion, and all of which produce very similar symptoms to those from which Miss Bankes suffered, might have been given by Smethurst in order to terminate the pregnancy of Miss Bankes? This point was never raised at the trial, and no analyses were conducted to prove the presence or absence of any of these drugs.

All these facts do undoubtedly minimize, if they do not do away with, the chain of circumstantial evidence, on which the prosecution relied, and which they endeavoured to prove. There was enough probability to support a conviction, and enough possibility to allow an acquittal, according as the evidence of the medical witnesses should determine the balance.

The next question is: did the testimony of the scientific witnesses prove that Miss Bankes died of poisoning? If it did, there could be no doubt that the hand which administered it was that of Smethurst.

I propose to examine this evidence (a) on the clinical, (b) on the pathological, and (c) on the toxicological side. Before doing this I shall briefly summarize the defence from a medical point of view.

A delicate fragile woman who had suffered from uterine disease, and used vaginal injections, who was one of a family subject to bilious attacks, who was herself the frequent subject of nausea and liable to occasional vomiting, marries at the age of forty-two. Between three and four months later she becomes pregnant, and about the same time, or about five to seven weeks before her death, she begins to suffer from vomiting and diarrhoea, which becomes exceedingly obstinate. Effervescing draughts with prussic acid, grey powder, Dover's powder, opiate enemeta, bismuth, acetate of lead and opium, nitrate of silver, sulphate of copper, are tried successively, and all prove useless. Some of them are even followed by an increase of symptoms. This goes on from 28 March to 3 May, when the patient dies, exhausted. The post-mortem shows a condition of the liver which explains the bilious attacks and a state of intestine which closely corresponds with the ordinary effects of acute dysentery. The uterus contains an ovum of from five to seven weeks' development, and there are none of the special lesions of the mouth, oesophagus, stomach, or anus which are looked for in irritant mineral poisoning. No arsenic is found in the body, and only from a quarter to half a grain of antimony. As there was no arsenic found, it could not have been a case of arsenic poisoning. The small quantity of antimony might have been given unknowingly as an impurity in the many metallic drugs administered. She could not have died of poisoning, therefore, while her death is explained in the simplest and most natural manner as a severe case of the vomiting associated with pregnancy, to be expected in a bilious delicate woman who had suffered from uterine disease and became pregnant for the first time at the age of forty-two.

Now, let us examine the evidence in this remarkable case.

(a) Clinical evidence. The testimony of the three doctors who attended Miss Bankes, and who were the only ones who had actually seen her alive and followed the symptoms of the patient from day to day, were all in favour of the disease being due to some form of irritant poisoning. Dr Julius certainly thought so, and sent his partner, Dr Bird, to see the patient. The latter attended her for a few days. No suspicion of poison arose in his mind, but, after Dr Julius had suggested it to him, he agreed with the diagnosis. Dr Todd, the consultant who was called in, and who saw the patient only once, just before death, also agreed. This is, of course, very important evidence, but it was suspicion only, nothing more.

The symptoms of arsenic poisoning are as follows: burning sensations in the throat and stomach, nausea and persistent vomiting, diarrhoea with blood, pain and tenderness in the abdomen, and extreme prostration. These correspond very closely indeed with the symptoms described by the doctors attending Miss Bankes. Antimony poisoning produces very similar results. It was contended by the medical men for the defence, from a description of the symptoms only, and not from any personal observations, that all these were consistent with the disturbances which occur in early pregnancy, especially if in association with an attack of dysentery. Pregnancy, especially in those who are having their first baby, frequently produces vomiting sometimes so severe that it ends fatally. It is usually accompanied by constipation, sometimes by diarrhoea. But in spite of this superficial resemblance of the symptoms to those of Miss Bankes, and in spite of the evidence of some of the witnesses for the defence, notably Dr Tyler Smith, it does not appear to me that this case in any way resembles a severe case of the vomiting of pregnancy. If we imagine dysentery in addition, as was suggested for Smethurst, it is possible to account for the symptoms in this way, but then we have to explain the whole case by invoking two distinct and separate pathologies, always an unsafe plan in medicine. I think one must conclude, from the clinical evidence, that the case was remarkably like one of irritant poisoning, and was not merely a severe case of the vomiting of pregnancy, complicated by dysentery, though I do not think it would be possible definitely to deny the latter.

(b) The pathological appearances found were as follows: the uterus contained a foetus of from five to seven weeks' duration. The oesophagus was healthy. The stomach at the pyloric end was red, in the centre pale, at the cardiac end dark coloured. There were no ulcers, no perforation, no signs of acute inflammation. The duodenum was inflamed for about three inches. In the ileum (part of the small intestine) the mucous membrane was greatly altered at the lower three feet. It was thickened and roughened. In the caecum (part of the large intestine) were inflammation, ulceration, and sloughing. Those appearances lessened lower down. In the colon there was still ulceration, but in a lesser degree.

In arsenic poisoning it is well recognized that the most important indications are those presented by the stomach and intestines. In the stomach the mucous membrane is intensely inflamed. Parts only may be attacked. There may be haemorrhages. Sometimes, when arsenic in a soluble form has been given, the inflamed appearance is not present. It was absent in the case of Miss Bankes, with the exception of one part, where there was a distinct haemorrhage. The upper part of the small intestine presents similar appearances to the stomach, but there is not usually any severe inflammation or ulceration of this part of the bowel. In antimonial poisoning, of which there are not a great number of cases recorded, the appearance of the mucous membrane of the stomach and intestine is similar to that produced by arsenic. (In the *Bravo* case, in 1876, tartar emetic, which is a salt of antimony, was used. Here the stomach and intestines were pale, but there was ulceration of the caecum, and the large intestine was blood-stained, signs very like those in the present case.) In dysentery it is mainly the large intestine which is affected with ulceration and inflammation. In the words of Dr Wilks, who was one of the witnesses for the prosecution, 'It is impossible not to recognize the resemblance which the present case bears to the latter form of dysentery, a form characterized by an acute inflammation of the whole mucous membrane, terminating in sloughing, and with effusion of blood from the surface, and especially resembling those cases which have terminated by a peritonitis.'

From the pathological aspect, then, I think no conclusions can be drawn. The appearances might or might not have been caused by irritant poison; they might or might not have been caused by dysentery.

(c) Chemical evidence. The chemical evidence was of the very utmost importance. Dr Taylor discovered a minute quantity of antimony in blood from the heart, traces in the large and small bowel, and in one kidney. In no other viscus was any found. No arsenic was discovered anywhere in the body. A small quantity of this poison was found in one motion examined before death, none whatever in any of the viscera. This was the result of the careful examination by a skilled toxicologist of the body of a woman who was said to have been killed by the continuous administration of two metallic poisons, arsenic and antimony, for several weeks.

I think the possibility of arsenical poisoning can be dismissed at once. The sole chemical evidence was the finding of arsenic by Dr Taylor in one motion before death. If this were really present, it could, possibly, have been accounted for by impurities in some of the many metallic drugs administered. Although those from the surgery of Dr Julius were examined and said to contain no arsenic, evidence was given that bismuth, obtained from the same wholesale house as that from which Dr Julius obtained his drugs, was found to contain arsenic. But the great probability is that Dr Taylor was mistaken in his analysis. His whole evidence was considerably discredited by a very serious error made by him in his examination of the bottle. In the house of Dr Smethurst had been found various vessels, some forty in number. These were all analysed by Dr Taylor. In only one (the celebrated 'bottle No. 21') did he find any evidence of poison. Dr Taylor swore in the lower Courts that he had discovered arsenic in this. He subsequently found that the arsenic was due to an impurity in the copper gauze, used in the tests he made. The instrument employed for detection had itself furnished the poison. Before the trial he recognized his mistake and notified both the prosecution and the defence. But the fact remains that he had made such a grave error that if it had not been discovered in time it would naturally have told very seriously against the prisoner. Arsenic would have been found in his possession, which would have been a point favouring his guilt.

Dr Taylor acknowledged he had used the same materials for the testing of the motion as he had for the bottle. We may therefore conclude that this result also was due to impurities in the material used. It is impossible to imagine that, if arsenic had been the cause of death, it should have been present in one motion only, and not at all in any of the tissues of the body. Of all poisons, arsenic is probably the most easy of sure detection by a skilled chemist. Reinsch's test, that employed in this case, remains one of the best, and is still frequently used for the discovery of

DR THOMAS SMETHURST

arsenic, and it is certain that, as it yielded no arsenic when
applied to the viscera, none was present. Since the test for
arsenic in the tissues was first introduced by Rose in 1808,
there is no case of slow arsenical poisoning on record in
which the poison has not been found.

As regards the small amount of antimony found in the
body, is there any other explanation of its presence? One
would expect, if death had been due to this cause, that the
antimony would have been found to be much more ex-
tensively distributed than it was. It should undoubtedly
have been present in considerable quantity in the liver.
This is the organ where it is most usually stored in cases of
poison. But none was found there. Various drugs, such as
bismuth, which had been given to Miss Bankes, do contain
antimony as an impurity, and it is possible that the small
amount found, from one-quarter to one-half a grain, may
have been derived from this source.

It must also be remembered that no arsenic or antimony
was ever found in the possession of Smethurst, in his house,
or in any of the food. In all previous trials for poisoning
such questions as these were considered as of very great
importance. Even so long ago as a hundred years stress was
laid on this. In all cases of this kind the basis upon which
the prosecution rested was the possession of poison by the
accused. Unless this were proved, conviction was impossible.
Donellan himself distilled the laurel water which he gave to
Sir Theodosius Broughton; Mary Blandy confessed to receiving from her lover the powders which she gave to her
father; Tawell bought the prussic acid, and Palmer the
strychnine, which they used to murder their victims.

Totalling all these arguments on one side or the other,
can it possibly be said that death by poisoning was proved?
The symptoms observed during life are perfectly compatible
with – more than that, are very strongly suggestive of –
irritant poisoning. They are those usually observed in such

cases. But they are also compatible with, though less suggestive of, the diseases put forward by the defence, namely, dysentery, with the addition of vomiting due to pregnancy. The pathological findings can be accounted for on either hypothesis. There is very little balance one way or the other. The chemical evidence is very definitely against arsenical poisoning, and not at all conclusive in favour of antimonial poisoning. No modern toxicologist would dream of considering the facts proved in the case of Smethurst on this point as conclusive of this condition.

In my opinion, the evidence, both circumstantial and scientific, completely failed to prove the guilt of Smethurst. There were, of course, many very suspicious circumstances; but, reviewing the facts as a whole, especially considering the absence of an adequate motive and the failure to find any arsenic and merely a trace of antimony in the body (the prosecution itself recognized how weak was its position on this point, for Mr Serjeant Ballantine, in his concluding address to the jury, said, 'It was not pretended to say positively that the death was occasioned either by antimony or by arsenic; all they said was that death was occasioned by some poison or other'), I think that, however suspicious certain facts undoubtedly were, a verdict of not guilty should and would have been returned but for the lamentable error of Dr Taylor, which prejudiced the case throughout. Had there been in existence at that time a Court of Criminal Appeal, I am convinced it would have reversed the finding of the jury.

*

On Saturday, 12 November, to the astonishment of everyone, Smethurst was brought up at Southwark Police Court from Horsemonger Lane Jail and charged with bigamy. This was before he had received his pardon. Evidence was called to prove the bigamy, after which Mr Combe, the magistrate, asked Mr Robinson, who appeared for the defence, whether he had any remarks to make.

Mr Robinson: Knowing sir, that you will send the prisoner for trial, I, on his part, reserve his defence. I wish, however, to ask, as the prisoner is fully prepared, whether you, sir, will admit him to bail? Security can be given to any amount.

Mr Combe: He is brought here, Mr Keene, is he not, by you, on a writ of *habeas corpus*?

Mr Keene: He is, sir.

Mr Combe: Then he cannot be released on bail.

Mr Robinson: I am expecting a pardon for the prisoner from the charge for which he is at present in custody, and then the present would be a bailable offence.

Mr Combe: It will be quite time enough when the prisoner is pardoned for you to make your application. I now fully commit the prisoner for trial.

On Thursday 17 November, as soon as Mr Combe took his seat on the bench, Mr Robinson said that he had now to propose bail for Dr Smethurst.

Mr Combe: I can't accept bail. You know that, Mr Robinson.

Mr Robinson: You were pleased to say on Saturday that if a free pardon were granted to my client you might accept bail.

Mr Combe: I said that, under the circumstances before me. Where is your free pardon?

Mr Robinson: I have it here, sir.

The following is a copy:

The Seal of Our Lady the Queen, 'Victoria R'.

Whereas, Thomas Smethurst was, at a session of the Central Criminal Court, holden in August last, convicted upon a certain indictment then and there preferred against him for the wilful murder of Isabella Bankes, and had sentence of death passed upon him for the same, We, in consideration of some circumstances, humbly represented unto us, are graciously pleased to extend our grace and mercy unto him, the said Thomas Smethurst, and to grant him a free pardon for the crime of which he stands so convicted upon such indictment as aforesaid.

Our will and pleasure, therefore, is, that you take due notice thereof, and for doing so this will be your warrant.

Given at our Court of St James, the 14th day of November, 1859, in the 23rd year of our reign.

To our trusty friend and well beloved our justices of the Central Criminal Court, the High Sheriff of the county of Surrey, and all others whom it may concern.

By her Majesty's commands,

G. C. Lewis

Mr Combe: I have read that, but at the same time I can't take bail.

Mr Robinson: I have his brother, a wealthy gentleman, and an ex-M.P., who will be answerable for him.

Mr Combe: I tell you I cannot accept bail. Whatever the Government has done, I have to do my duty as a magistrate. This man is charged with bigamy.

Mr Robinson: But you have power to accept bail in such cases.

Mr Combe: In this case I will not. Go to a judge in chambers if you like.

Mr Robinson: Then you refuse to accept bail here, sir?

Mr Combe: Yes, certainly. I cannot interfere.

There is not very much of interest in the trial of Smethurst for bigamy, but an observation of the judge is worth repeating, it is so very applicable to this and many other cases. The learned judge, Mr Baron Bramwell, interposed when Smethurst's counsel made the observation that the prisoner had been proved to be innocent of the crime of murder. He stated that pardon was no more a certificate of innocence than a verdict of not guilty. The prisoner was sentenced to one year's imprisonment with hard labour.

Some two years after his release he brought an action to prove the will of the woman whom he had been convicted of poisoning, and actually won it. The jury decided that the will was valid, and thus ended the series of trials in which Smethurst figured.

Alfred Arthur Rouse

· 1931 ·

BY

HELENA NORMANTON

AT about 2 a.m. in the morning of 6 November 1930, two young men were returning from a dance to their homes at Hardingstone, near Northampton. William Bailey and Alfred Thomas Brown were cousins. The weekly Thursday dance had been brought forward from the sixth to the fifth to make it a celebration of the night dedicated to the Gunpowder Plot.

Hardingstone is a village with a population of about nine hundred, an easy walk from Northampton. To reach it the cousins had to walk along the Northampton to London main road until they came to a left turning known as Hardingstone Lane. A motor-car flashed by on the main road to London. After its sudden glare and noise the pedestrians at the corner, just behind it, must have been practically invisible, and just as they were turning into that lane they observed two things almost simultaneously. A hatless man was apparently climbing from the ditch by the hedge almost on the corner of the road opposite to them, and a bright red glow was rising above the hedge some way up the lane in front of them. 'What's the blaze?' Mr Bailey asked his cousin. The man, who by that time had crossed over and was retreating just at their rear, as if answering him, said: 'It looks as if some one has had a bonfire.' They noticed that he spoke as if he were out of breath, and, curiously enough, after he had passed them.

The cousins walked homewards and onwards in the direction of the glare, while the hatless man continued to go towards the main road. Looking round at him they observed that, having now reached the junction of the lane and the main road, the man did not seem certain of his direction. He took a few steps to the right towards Northampton, turned towards London, and then hesitated in the middle of the road. When they last saw him he was watching them as they ran towards the huge bonfire whose flames were leaping some fifteen feet high. It would certainly have caused them great surprise if they had then realized that their chance meeting with the hatless man was destined to be the strongest link in a chain of circumstances which was to bring him to the gallows in one of the most unusual and sensational crimes of modern times – the Blazing Car Mystery.

In all probability it was that accidental encounter which caused the hatless man suddenly to change his entire plan. The moon happened to be so bright that his general appearance could be remarkably well observed, and, if need be, described, a fact which Alfred Arthur Rouse must instantly have realized. He had just left the scene of a calculated murder, because of which an unknown man was at that moment being shrivelled up in the furnace of Rouse's lighted car. If, as has been widely thought, the burnt-up corpse was intended to be taken for his own, the appearance of a man at the material time who could and would be described as having precisely his own style, clothing, and physique, would be a decided impediment to the success of the scheme. People might not be prepared to believe that it was the owner-driver of the car who had accidentally perished. The insurance company might be led to make close inquiries. The few steps taken by Rouse in the direction of Northampton were, one takes it, part of his original plan, a flight north away from all old haunts. The hesitation and the return probably marked his rapid abandonment of that plan.

The remaining four months of the life of Alfred Rouse were devoted to vain and pitiable attempts to escape the inevitable consequences of the fact that Mr Bailey and Mr Brown turned into Hardingstone Lane a few seconds too soon to suit him. Luck had not been with him. If only he had lain down in that ditch so that they passed without seeing him! If only he had realized that on the left of the nearside hedge was a meadow which he could safely have crossed without leaving footprints, instead of mistaking it, in the moonlight, for a dangerous ploughed field, as he did!

*

For the moment we will stay with Brown and Bailey. As they neared the blaze they saw that it framed a motor-car around and in which flames were furiously leaping some fifteen feet high. Nothing was discernible inside the car. They ran on into the village; Bailey called out his father, who happened to be the village constable, and he brought along Police Constable Copping. By the time Copping arrived the flames had lessened to a height of five or six feet, so they could approach nearer. Soon, by the light of Mr Brown's electric torch, something like a ball could be seen, and as the flames lowered a body became visible, of which the 'ball' was the head. Buckets of water were sent for, the fire was extinguished in about twelve minutes, and it was then seen that the car was almost completely burnt out. Police Inspector Lawrence was sent for, and careful observations were made.

So much turned at the trial upon the exact position in which the charred corpse was found that it was a great misfortune that photographs of it were not, immediately daylight came, taken *in situ*. The matter was not altogether an easy one for the Northampton police to handle, for Hardingstone Lane is by no means so unfrequented a thoroughfare as its name would imply. It is a well-made road, eighteen feet wide, along which five bus routes run. Naturally, the police would feel it desirable to clear away the car and debris from the road's metalled surface as soon as possible, and even stronger reasons would apply to the removal of so grim an object as the burnt corpse. Nevertheless, it was unfortunate that no medically trained witness even saw it before removal. In the absence of skilled observation upon the point, the Court had to fall back upon the less precise observations of the police.

The evidence of Police Constable Copping (given from his recollection, not from notes) established that the corpse was face downwards, the head in the driver's seat, the trunk lying across the other seat. The right arm appeared to be stretched as if over the back of the passenger's seat, but was burnt off at the elbow. The left arm could not be seen before removal. The left leg was doubled up underneath the trunk. The right leg appeared to be extended, but was burnt off at the knee. A charred boot heel was found six inches to the left of the left-side running board of the car, in a line with the driver's seat, lying out on the roadside, just on the edge of the grass verge. Apparently Copping did not think at the time that the position of the body mattered very much. He gave evidence at the Police Court that 'the body did not quite look as if the person had been sitting in the passenger's seat and fallen forwards into the driver's seat.'

Police Constable Valentine, who arrived with Inspector Lawrence at 3.10 a.m., gave similar evidence, with a little more precision about the right leg – that it was extended where the running-board had been and was sticking out of the remains of the chassis about eight inches, with the foot burnt off at about the ankle. At about 3.40 a.m. the body was removed by the officers.

Inspector Lawrence, who had arrived on the scene at 3.10 a.m., corroborated the evidence of Police Constables Copping and Valentine but described the position of the right arm in a slightly different manner – it was extended upwards to about the height of the back of the passenger's seat, but the back of the seat at that time had fallen away, the seat having been burnt down to the springs. The right leg had gone from about half-way between the ankle and the knee. According to this officer it was at 4.40 a.m. that the body was actually removed from the car. It was taken, wrapped in sacking, into a garage of the Crown Inn at Hardingstone, and later to the Northampton General Hospital.

Of the three police officers who saw the body immediately after death, one saw that the right leg was burnt off at the knee, another that it had gone about half-way between ankle and knee, and the third that it had burnt off at the ankle. Probably none of these witnesses had seen a similarly burnt body before, and each tried to be as accurate as possible about a material thing foreign to his usual sphere of observation, something indeed which any non-medical witness might find difficult to describe. The discrepancies, however, further a natural regret that neither a written note, photographs, nor immediate medical evidence were available later for the assistance of the Court and jury.

But up to this point there was nothing to suggest to the police that a crime had necessarily been committed. To them it no doubt seemed that an accidental fire had occurred, which would certainly be followed by an inquest and possibly by inquiries connected with the insurance of the car. They therefore removed the debris of the car from the road to the grass verge, and circulated a statement that the police were anxious to get into touch with a man aged between thirty and thirty-five, height 5ft 10ins., with a round, small face and curly black hair, wearing a light mackintosh and dark trousers, hatless, and carrying an attaché case. In the course of their inquiries every hotel and inn in Northampton was visited.

The daily papers on 7 November 1930 contained illustrations of the burnt-out car and the story of the hatless man; among them the *Daily Sketch*. Early in the afternoon of 6 November two plain clothes officers had called upon Mrs Rouse at her home in Buxted Road, Finchley, having traced it by means of the registered number of the car MU 1468, and had requested her to go to Northampton. These facts were common to all the Press on 7 November.

It can be inferred that the police expected valuable assistance from Mrs Rouse by way of identification of the parts of the debris. Accordingly, she went on 6 November, but was not allowed to see the charred body itself; she stated to the police (according to her interview as given in the *Daily Sketch* on 5 February 1931) that 'brace buckles and pieces of clothing . . . *might* be his' (i.e. her husband's), after viewing what the police did show her.

*

In the meantime, where was Rouse? If he had gone straight into Northampton Police Station directly after he had met Brown and Bailey and told a plausible story of a distressing fire, it is not unlikely that he might be walking the earth today. He had missed *the* piece of conduct most conducive to belief in his innocence by trying to mislead Brown and Bailey into thinking it was a mere Guy Fawkes blaze and by not asking them to return and help him put it out. His next best course would have been to report the event immediately to the police and the company insuring the car. Alternatively, he might have tried to carry out his presumed original plan and fade away, gambling on the chances against any conclusive identification of himself by means of any descriptions that Brown and Bailey could furnish. That would have involved going at once to some place where no one had ever seen him before.

But while the police were of necessity concentrating upon

the car itself and its grim contents, Rouse was consistently doing everything possible to ensure his own ultimate execution. He played the part neither of an innocent man nor of one carrying out his own guilty plan, but an extraordinary jumble of both.

At this point it becomes imperative to consider why Alfred Arthur Rouse should have felt it advantageous to set his own motor-car on fire, and what possible benefit it could be to him for the world to believe he had been burnt to death in it. These points cannot be understood without going back upon the life story of this extraordinary man.

Alfred Arthur Rouse was of Irish extraction on his mother's side, and was born on 6 April 1894. He was the son of a respectable hosier of Milkwood Road, Herne Hill, and was one of three children. In 1900 the household was disrupted, and Mr W. E. Rouse placed his children under the care of his sister. Young Arthur Rouse was educated at a local council school, where he gave promise of being a keen, athletic, courageous, and bright boy. When he left he learnt carpentry, and attended evening classes to study the piano, mandoline, and violin. He sang well, and, when adult, possessed a pleasing baritone voice, although his speaking voice was high-pitched and unconvincing.

After a short spell as office boy in an estate agent's, young Rouse obtained a position with a soft-furnishing goods house in the West End, where he remained for five years. He also became a sacristan at St Saviour's Church, Stoke Newington. He enlisted for service in the Great War on 8 August 1914 and was drafted as Private 2011 into the Queen's Territorial Regiment. Before he was sent out to France he married on 29 November 1914 a young woman clerk named Lily May Watkins, at St Saviour's Church, St Albans, he being then twenty and his wife twenty-three. He was sent to France on 15 March 1915, and on 25 May 1915 he was severely wounded in head, thigh, and leg by a shell-burst at Festubert, and sent back. An operation was performed on the left side of his head, and for many months he remained a war-shattered invalid. As a patient he was brave, uncomplaining, and cheerful. One of the hospitals where he was cared for was Harewood House, Yorkshire. Eventually he returned to his wife, discharged in 1916 as no longer fit for active service.

Up to this point in his life there is little on record but what is to the credit of Rouse, except that a son now being reared in Paris owed his existence to Rouse's sojourn there in 1915. But now a change appears. He obtained various outdoor employments, and, on the whole, constantly improved his position. Aided by a facile tongue and extremely good looks, he eventually became a commercial traveller, who at the time of his crime was earning approximately five hundred pounds a year. He had bought several motor-cars in succession and had become a skilled mechanic and driver. The life he led took him rapidly about the country and formed an ideal background for philandering with all the young women with whom a commercial traveller's life so easily brings him into contact. Tobacconists' assistants, shopgirls, probationer nurses, chambermaids, and so on, readily fell victim to his plausible tongue, ingratiating manners, handsome appearance, and fantastic lies.

Needless to remark, in the account of himself he gave to these girls, he was always a person of some social prominence. He had been a major in the war. The absent mother, for whose caress he had so yearned as a boy (one of his effective and pathetic touches in his numerous courtships), reappeared in his fairy tales concerning his youth as a lovely flashing woman, clothed most exquisitely. He had naturally been at Eton and Cambridge, not anywhere so ordinary as a local Board school. He was a superb practitioner in the art of telling the tale to precisely the type of girl whose great ambition is to marry a man a few grades above her class. So long as girls of that type read, think as they do think, and spin their fantastic daydreams, the Landrus, Mahons, Smiths, and Rouses of this life will flourish.

As Rouse improved his circumstances, he moved from one place to another until finally, about 1927, he and his wife went to live in a small £750 house they had started to buy in Buxted Road, Finchley. Whenever Rouse's work allowed him to be at home, he tried to improve his house and garden. Like Mahon, whom he resembled in many ways, he soon became a popular figure in the little social circle of his neighbourhood; the hero of the communal tennis courts.

In 1920 a fourteen-year-old Edinburgh girl named Helen Campbell became a member of a household where Rouse was a frequent visitor, and by the time the girl was fifteen she had borne a child to him in a home for unmarried mothers. The child was born on 21 October 1921 but fortunately died when only five weeks old, after which the mother returned to her duties. Rouse renewed the association and Miss Campbell became pregnant a second time, whereupon Rouse, who posed to her as a single man, induced her to go through a ceremony of marriage which she believed valid and he, of course, knew to be bigamous. This marriage was at St Mary's Church, Islington, and took place in November 1924. After it the couple lived in Liverpool Road, Islington, where, on 22 July, a son was born to them. To this child Rouse was a devotedly loving father. Throughout what she believed to be her marriage Miss Campbell maintained herself, but her acceptance of one position in a restaurant was not agreeable to Rouse; after a difference of opinion they parted, she keeping the boy. The position proving financially unsatisfactory, Miss Campbell was obliged to bring proceedings against Rouse for the maintenance of the boy, which she did at the Guildhall on 17 October 1929, when an order was made for him to pay ten shillings a week. It is remarkable that at the hearing he not only readily admitted the paternity, but expressed great fondness of and desire for children. His payments on the order were, however, very irregular.

Subsequently it was arranged, after a meeting between Mrs Rouse and Helen Campbell, that the boy should be reared, on certain conditions, in the Rouse home; and that in fact was the state of affairs at the time of the destruction of the car, so far as Helen Campbell was concerned. She saw her son occasionally, for Rouse motored him over to see her. The child was well and kindly treated by Mrs Rouse, who did her best to make the little boy happy and to patch up the strange situation.

Early in 1925 Rouse became acquainted with a young domestic servant, a Miss Nellie Tucker, then in a position at Hendon. She was a bright, humorous girl, aged seventeen, and Rouse added her to his retinue, taking her about with him to hotels. Naturally, he posed to her as a single man, and informed her that he lived in rooms in Gillingham Street, Victoria. He actually had an accommodation address at Gillingham Street at which he received numerous letters for some years. He promised Nellie Tucker marriage at the elusive date when trade should have improved. On 2 May 1928 a girl was born to Nellie Tucker, in respect of whom a further maintenance order was obtained against Rouse in November 1928. Here again his payments were irregular. The child was put out to a foster-mother for a fee of twelve and sixpence a week.

On 29 October 1930, about a week before the crime, Nellie Tucker gave birth to a second girl child by Rouse at the City of London Maternity Hospital, City Road, London. On the evening of the crime itself soon after 7 o'clock Rouse went to see Nellie Tucker and left her at

8 p.m. Nellie Tucker subsequently described him as being very depressed and worried-looking upon that occasion. He told her he feared he might lose his job, and seemed annoyed at hearing how soon she had to leave hers; probably because he realized it would mean finding other accommodation for her sooner than he had been anticipating. It also appeared to Nellie Tucker that he had been keeping an anxious eye on the clock during the whole hour of his call, as if he had an appointment. 'Are you meeting any one?' she asked. He looked at her vacantly and said, 'No' He then confessed that he had so many things to pay that he hardly knew where to turn. Telling her that he had to go north that night on business, he left her.

Not only had he to go north, he had to go west, although poor Nellie Tucker did not know that, for another girl in her teens, Ivy Jenkins, was lying pregnant and very ill in her parents' home at Gellygaer, in Monmouthshire. She had informed her father, a colliery proprietor, that she had been married to Rouse for some months. Rouse had visited the house as her husband, and had led all the family to believe that he had paid £125 for a house at Kingston, which he had furnished beautifully for his bride. On 6 November he was due to take her to that home. Of course it was as much fantasy as most of his other stories. But Ivy Jenkins, alas for Rouse, was not quite the friendless, isolated little girl he had hitherto been lucky enough to meet. She had a fond father and an affectionate brother. What might they say or do if he could not take her away to the promised home? Furthermore, he had added to his worries by inviting her sister Phyllis to come and stay with them for their first three months in Kingston.

It is really difficult to conceive of any man of normal mentality getting himself into this maze of difficulty. But that was the position in which Rouse had placed himself at that moment. There were other women in his life at

Birmingham, Southampton, and elsewhere, but if their claims were insistent at this time not so much is known of the matter. There was a child in Paris and another in an English county. Broadly speaking, Rouse was rapidly approaching the point when outgoings on irregular *ménages* would utterly cripple him, to say nothing of the fact that he had to pay at the rate of £1 12s. per week on his car, and £1 7s. 6d. to his building society. He gave his wife £2 a week for housekeeping, and, whenever the child was with her, another ten shillings a week.

Mr and Mrs Rouse had been considering by November 1930 whether they would sell their house and separate, he to make her an allowance. To all their friends they still appeared to be on good terms, a devoted couple, but it would have been astonishing if Mrs Rouse had not become disillusioned as a result of all her husband's infidelities. Helen Campbell and Nellie Tucker she knew of, and she had found Ivy Jenkins's photograph in her husband's pocket.

Nor perhaps was this monetary situation the sum total of his troubles. A braggart, as Rouse was, boasting of his conquests to the other commercial travellers he met, was laying himself open, sooner or later, to the attentions of any blackmailer who might choose to take his affairs in hand. Miss Jenkins recorded her conviction that such was indeed the case. All the women who had these tragic associations with him agreed on one characteristic of Rouse – his overweening vanity. Every one who had any dealings with him testified to his excessive and boastful loquacity. He could not even pay an instalment on his car without boasting about his exceptionally unfettered conditions of employment. And like so many men whose standards in sexual morality are low, Rouse was immune from the companionable masculine traits; he neither drank nor smoked. Significantly enough, other men had no use for him.

*

Rouse, as he left the two men at the corner of Hardingstone Lane, had not only the blazing horror on his mind; he had all these other pressing worries to consider. It has been stated that his original plan was, after burning up the unknown man in his car, to walk through Northampton and make his way to Scotland. There he might have lain concealed round and about Glasgow, of which he had probably heard plenty from Helen Campbell, who had lived there in her childhood.

If he could only have obtained funds he might have tried to get out to New Zealand or the South Sea Islands, places he had often praised to Ivy Jenkins. If he could not disguise himself sufficiently, perhaps no place would have been safer than a different part of his own country. Gellygaer itself was certainly the most inaccessible of all spots he actually frequented, and a timely local investment for a few hundred pounds, or even £1,000, had been discussed and was open to him there. If he settled down in Gellygaer there would be little need to produce the beautifully furnished, mythical house at Kingston.

Be that as it may, what he did choose to do was make a hasty dash back to London by getting a lift in a lorry, and then an equally rapid charabanc trip to the home of Ivy Jenkins in Gellygaer.

Whilst in London, he went first to his home in Buxted Road, arriving about 6.20 a.m., and staying there for something under half an hour. Rouse stated that he had no food at home, did not change his clothes, and that his purpose was 'to tell my wife not to be worried'. He did not state in evidence what cause his wife, who was at that time peacefully in bed, should have had to worry more than usual about anything he might do. Later on in the day she would no doubt have plenty to worry her, but, if it had not been for a mistake she made about the time, at least she would have been spared, by her husband's considerate return, from any idea that he was not alive and well up to about 7 a.m. on the morning of 6 November 1930 – for she admitted having heard him come in. It is, of course, very easy to mistake the time when one is awakened suddenly on a dark November morning; Mrs Rouse stated to the Press on 5 February 1931 that she thought his return was about one o'clock at night, when it was in fact between six and seven in the morning that Rouse came home. Although the police called at her home later in the day and broke the news of the tragedy at Northampton to her, she described herself in that interview as still imagining that the fire had happened in the portion of the night still remaining after his departure. Before Mrs Rouse left for Northampton on 6 November she said, according to a report in the *Daily Express* on 7 November, 'I have had many conflicting messages. I do not know whether it is my husband who is dead in the car or not.' According to the same newspaper, issue of 8 November: 'Mrs Rouse has informed the authorities she has had no word from her husband'; and in view of her mistake about the time, of course she thought she had not had any word of him. She did not put the time as late as in fact it was.

Whether Rouse did or did not use this brief visit home to change his clothing was never formally proved. Owing to the fact that New Scotland Yard was not officially called in, the house was never searched nor was Rouse's complete wardrobe examined.

At Gellygaer he saw in the *Daily Sketch* on 7 November the account of the burnt-out car, his own description as the hatless man, and an account of the visit to his wife by the police and her alleged trip to Northampton. Realizing that the minute the Jenkinses saw the paragraph about his wife his whole position would be exposed to them, he hastily left for London, again by motor coach. One of the men who had driven Rouse from Gellygaer to Cardiff was apparently not satisfied by Rouse's remarks about his car, and mentioned the matter to a Cardiff journalist, who communicated with the local police. Before Rouse had even alighted from this last coach, two plain clothes officers were awaiting him, and invited him to accompany them to the Hammersmith Police Station, an invitation which effectively opened the final chapter of his story.

*

The sudden appearance of the plain clothes men by the motor coach at 9.20 p.m. on 7 November on Hammersmith Bridge was no doubt a great shock to Rouse. Under its impulse he said: 'Very well; I am glad it's all over. I was going to Scotland Yard about it. I am responsible. I am very glad it is over; I have had no sleep.'

At the Hammersmith Police Station Sergeant Skelly told him that the Northampton police wanted to interview him, and Rouse replied: 'I suppose they wish to see me about it. I don't know what happened exactly. I picked the man up on the Great North Road; he asked me for a lift. He seemed a respectable man, and said he was going to the Midlands. I gave him a lift. It was just this side of St Albans. He got in and I drove off, and after going some distance I lost my way. A policeman spoke to me about my lights. I did not know anything about the man, and I thought I saw his hand on my case which was in the back of the car. I later became sleepy and could hardly keep awake. The engine started to spit, and I thought I was running out of petrol. I pulled into the side of the road. I wanted to relieve myself, and said to the man: "There is some petrol in the can; you can empty it into the tank while I am gone," and lifted up the bonnet and showed him where to put it in. He said "What about a smoke?" I said: "I have given you all my cigarettes as it is." I then went some distance along the road, and had just got my trousers up quickly and ran towards the car which was in flames. I saw the man inside and tried to open the door, but could not, as the car was then a mass of flames. I then began to tremble violently. I was all of a shake. I did not know what to do, and ran as hard as I could along the road where I saw the two men. I felt I was responsible for what had happened. I lost my head and did not know what to do, and really don't know what I have done since.'

Sergeant Skelly asked if he had rescued the attaché case he then had with him, and Rouse answered that he had seen the man's hand on it when it was in the back of the car, so he took it with him when he got out.

At 1 a.m. Superintendent Brumby and Inspector Lawrence of the Northampton County Police arrived. The superintendent cautioned Rouse, and then there began the proceeding that must be agonizing for any guilty man, the taking of his voluntary statement. Let a man have committed all the crimes of the Borgias, Nero, and Henry VIII combined, it is still possible to feel a pang of sympathy for him at having to make a statement lasting from 1 a.m. at night till half past five in the morning, even with one break for a cup of tea, in the dreary surroundings of a police station.

Substantially, however, Rouse's account remained the same. He was well out of sight of the car when on fire. He did not know how it got on fire. He asked the man to pour petrol into the tank. There had been talk about a smoke just before he went away to evacuate. He could do nothing by the time he got back. Everything said or done or omitted afterwards was attributable to his state of panic. If all the circumstantial evidence had corroborated or, at any rate, not conflicted with this story, it should have stood a good sporting chance before the average jury. Every motorist has met the interfering fool in a car, and few of us have not encountered the smoker who is criminally careless about what he does with his cigarette and match ends. After a run from London to Northampton any driver would naturally want to leave a car for the purpose alleged. All this was plausible. All this could have happened to any good-natured motorist who had given a lift to a stranger.

Rouse had had nearly forty-four hours in which to think out his narration. Had he left it there, things might not have been so bad for him. But after the completion of the statement the officers brought Rouse back to Angel Lane Police Station at Northampton, where they all arrived at 9.30 a.m. on Saturday, 8 November. After breakfast he was detained in the office of Inspector Lawrence, and thought fit to ask that officer when the inquest was to be held on the deceased man. He was told at noon, and inquired whether his wife would be present, and asked if he could see her. On the inspector stating that he could do so later, Rouse made the following remarkable statement:

'She is already too good for me. I like a woman who will make a fuss of me. I don't ever remember my wife sitting on my knee, but otherwise she is a good wife. I am friendly with several women, but it is a very expensive game. I was on my way to Leicester on Wednesday when it happened, to hand in my slip on Thursday morning to draw some money from my firm. I was then going to Wales for the week-end. My harem takes me several places and I am not at home a great deal, but my wife doesn't ask questions now. I was arranging to sell my house and furniture. I was then going to make an allowance to the wife. I think I should clear between £100 and £150 from the sale.'

This speech, given in evidence by the inspector at the Police Court proceedings on 16 December 1930 undoubtedly helped to seal the fate of Rouse. Next day all over the country there were newspaper placards on which there prominently figured the words HAREM and ROUSE in varying arrangements. From that moment the accused was accurately, but for the purpose of an unbiased trial unfairly, branded as a callously immoral man; one who, in the judgement of that man in the street who ultimately becomes the man in the jury box, richly deserved a hanging anyhow, and was just the sort of villain who could be relied upon to burn up his car and an out-of-work passenger in order to defraud insurance companies and stage his disappearance from his seduced victims.

Before elaborating this point, it will perhaps interest the reader to learn that Mrs Rouse was allowed to see her husband quite shortly after this statement. He entered the room crying, and embraced her affectionately. Not, one feels, in the least hypocritically, for he was in that dire plight when any familiar face would be a godsend. He told her not to worry; all she could do was to pray for him and sell their home, as they had intended, in order to provide funds for his defence. Rouse, invariably kind to women on little points, then asked the superintendent if his wife could have the 6s. 3½d. which was all he had on him. Manlike, he then requested her to buy him two books and an ounce of John Cotton tobacco, so that in fact the poor lady had only her bare fare to London, and had to walk from the terminus to her home in Friern Barnet.

She did in fact sell the house and went to work as a shop assistant in Northampton in order to maintain herself near him during his last few weeks on earth. She showed great courage.

*

On the 9, 10, and 27 November and 15 and 16 December 1930 Rouse was brought before the bench of Justices of the Peace for the County of Northampton, their chairman being Mr John B. E. Campion, J.P., Mr D. L. Finnemore, a member of the bar located at Birmingham, appeared for Rouse, instructed at first by Mr Lee Roberts, who later was

associated for the purposes of his defence with Messrs
Drell & Price, a well-known Northampton firm of Solicitors.
Mr G. R. Paling appeared on behalf of the Director of
Public Prosecutions. No less than six witnesses were prof-
fered in connexion with the details of Rouse's private life –
Helen Campbell, Nellie Tucker, Mary Teresa Casey,
William Jenkins, Phyllis Maud Jenkins, and Inspector Law-
rence. Mary Teresa Casey was a sister of the City of London
Maternity Hospital. William and Phyllis Jenkins were the
father and sister respectively of Ivy Jenkins, who was herself too ill to be present. Inspector Lawrence, *inter alia*,
deposed to the notorious 'harem' speech.

There has been voluminous and detailed controversy over
the admissibility of this portion of the evidence for the
prosecution. Sir Patrick Hastings, K.C., naturally made
the most of the point when appearing for Rouse before
the Court of Criminal Appeal. By the course adopted by the
prosecution, he argued, Rouse's character had been blazoned
abroad in such a way that anyone having an even moderate
view of the duties of citizenship must have regarded Rouse's
career with horror.

Sir Patrick further argued that, at the Police Court, Mr
Paling had opened in his speech matters which were absolutely dreadful when considered in connexion with the
whole principle of our law that evidence as to character
must not be adduced against a prisoner upon his trial; and,
secondly, that we live in a world where the assistance of the
Press is so afforded that the unsavoury elements in a man's
life shall be given the widest possible publicity. If that
evidence had been put against the prisoner at the Northampton Assizes, the Court of Criminal Appeal could not
have permitted a trial such as that to stand. Sir Patrick
suggested further that it was infinitely worse and more
dangerous to have such evidence at a Police Court opened,

objected to (as, of course, it had been by Mr D. L. Finnemore), pressed, admitted, and, of course, read everywhere. Every member of the jury knew every item of it, but what was the defence to do? Deal with it as if offered? The man had in fact been tried, only in a worse way – as if prejudged. A characteristically dry query by Mr Justice Avory as to how the prosecution could be blamed for introducing a statement by a prisoner indicated his opinion of the matter; yet a question later on put by the Lord Chief Justice to Crown counsel (Mr Norman Birkett, K.C., M.P.) indicated an opposite view-point. The Lord Chief Justice asked: 'Is it not unfortunate that evidence as to character should be given at a Police Court which is inadmissible at a trial?'

The answer of Mr Norman Birkett, that the Crown had decided not to call that evidence, did not go so far in answering the Lord Chief Justice's question as the next comment from Mr Justice Avory: 'If an accused person introduces detrimental matter, it is impossible to say that he may not have some motive in introducing it.' Mr Norman Birkett developed this point by saying that the evidence (i.e. of the harem speech) could have had relevance as explaining Rouse's movements up and down the country. The words: 'My journeys take me . . . my harem is very costly . . .', however damaging, might have been meant to explain a movement at night. The other evidence (i.e. as to illegitimate children) might have been relevant to the desirability of disappearance.

*

The attitude taken by Mr Norman Birkett at the Assizes was that the Crown, after anxious and prolonged consideration, had decided to omit the evidence of Helen Campbell and Ivy Jenkins, and to offer evidence from Nellie Tucker of a very formal nature only, viz., her name, address, occupation, the fact that she had known the prisoner for about five years, and that she had seen him last on 5 November at the Maternity Hospital; that he had come about 7.5 and left at 8 o'clock.

The depositions thus dealt with were as follows:

THIS DEPONENT HELEN CAMPBELL on her oath says: I live at . . . and am a waitress. I first met the accused in 1920. I gave birth to a child on 21 October 1921. It only lived five weeks. On 22 July 1925 I gave birth to another child, a male. The accused is the father. On 17 October 1929 I obtained an order in respect of the Guildhall Police Court against the accused. He made payments to me in respect of that child. They were irregular. In the summer of this year I parted with the baby to the accused on certain conditions. The child went to . . . where I saw it on several occasions. After the arrest of the prisoner the child came to live with me and is still with me.

HELEN CAMPBELL

THIS DEPONENT NELLIE TUCKER on her oath says: I live at . . . and am a domestic servant. I have known the accused for getting on for five years. I gave birth to a child on 2 May 1928. The accused is the father. He has contributed towards the maintenance of the child but not regularly. The last payment he made to me was November 1st this year. In November 1928 I obtained an order against him for the maintenance of the child. This was at the North London Police Court. On 29 October this year I gave birth to another child at the City of London Maternity Hospital, City Road, London. The accused is the father of that child. I last saw accused on 5 November. I was then in bed at the Maternity Hospital. He came about five minutes past seven in the evening and left at eight o'clock.

Cross-examined – I continued to be friendly with accused after birth of the first child. At the Police Court he admitted paternity and offered to pay 10s. a week. I went to the Court because at the time I was in an institution and was told I must go to the Court to get an order.

NELLIE TUCKER

A statement had been taken from Ivy Jenkins, but she

was not actually called at the Police Court because of the state of her health, so that the statement does not appear in any part of the public record of the trial.

The almost complete withdrawal of evidence by the Crown as to the moral character of the prisoner cut short the need for any discussion as to whether the evidence itself was or was not admissible. It is rather a pity, from the point of view of the student of law, that the matter was not fully argued. A certain amount of confusion arose in the public mind, and it was too hastily assumed in certain quarters, even in legal journals and by the barristers corresponding with lay newspapers, that there had been a judicial ruling that the evidence in question was in fact inadmissible. No such ruling was ever given.

The views which Mr Justice Talbot did express upon the admissibility of Nellie Tucker's evidence in the course of a short argument were:

1. That its only relevance was possibly as to the pecuniary position of the prisoner and as to the date.

2. That if, as Mr Finnemore contended, it had no connexion whatever with the alleged affair at Hardingstone Lane, that would be an absolutely sufficient ground of legal objection.

3. That as to the wide publicity given in the Court below: 'I cannot help that.' But the learned judge requested that the discussion then proceeding should not be reported in the Press.

4. That as to the calling of Nellie Tucker to prove anything at all, 'I should think you would ask her as little as you can. The jury cannot help forming some conclusion.' In the course of the short argument, Mr Norman Birkett remarked: 'It was thought at one time – and I express no view – that it might be relevant upon the question of motive.'

It was a pity to put Nellie Tucker into the witness-box at all. To hear her name called would recall to the minds of the jury all the prisoner's irregular relations with women. The jury were, of course, sent to their room during the above legal discussion but what can one suppose they would be talking about during their retirement if not the prisoner's relations with various women thus brought to their recollection?

If motive had been abandoned by the Crown in connexion with this witness, a date was all she could legitimately give, and there never was any dispute as to the date Rouse left London, nor was there any remarkable conflict about the time of his departure from his home, which he himself placed at about 9.15 p.m. The prosecution, having verified for their own satisfaction that he was in the City Road, London, until 8 p.m., seem to have called Nellie Tucker somewhat needlessly. It would have been otherwise if Rouse, among the innumerable lies he had told, had inaccurately stated that he began his journey at some hour before 8 p.m., so that Nellie Tucker's evidence was necessary to disprove that time. It is very difficult to see how her evidence advanced the Crown's case at all at the Assizes, once the Crown had abandoned the aid of all Rouse's mistresses as relevant to motive. The earlier Rouse began his journey from London the worse it was for him, because it left too much time to make the four-hour journey to Northampton look a normal and ordinary one. He took, on his own chronology, two hours from Tally Ho corner to Markyate, a distance of some twenty miles. What was happening in that two hours? Presumably a good deal more than just the mere drive which was all he thought fit to admit either in examination-in-chief or in cross-examination; even if a slow one to bring his crime within the small hours. Unless the Crown wished the jury so to infer, the positive evidence of the journey could have rested on P.C. Lilley's encounter with Rouse's car, amplified by Rouse's own voluntary statement.

Upon the technical side of the question whether Rouse's immoral career was admissible or not to prove motive, the general rule is, of course, that nothing may be given in evidence which does not directly tend to the proof or disproof of matters at issue. The leading case is *Makin* v. *Attorney-General for N.S.W.* [1894] A.C. 57, where it was laid down that:

> The mere fact that evidence adduced tends to show the commission of other crimes does not render it inadmissible if it be relevant to an issue before the jury, and it may be so relevant if it bears on the question whether the acts alleged to constitute the crime charged in the indictment were designed or accidental, or to rebut a defence which would be otherwise open to the accused.

Neither on the true construction of Section 423 of the Criminal Law Amendment Act of 46 Vict. c. 17 (New South Wales) is a higher Court empowered to affirm a conviction where the evidence submitted to the jury was inadmissible and may have influenced the verdict. (Merely formal matter not bearing directly on the guilt or innocence of the accused is an exception to this.)

> It is undoubtedly not competent for the prosecution to adduce evidence tending to show that the accused had been guilty of criminal acts other than those covered by the indictment, for the purpose of leading to the conclusion that the accused is a person likely from his conduct or character to have committed the offence for which he is to be tried.

The very case which lays down these clear principles also states that it

> may be often very difficult to draw the line and to decide whether a particular piece of evidence is on the one side or the other,

and that the decisions have not always been consistent.

It is perfectly obvious in Rouse's case that the prosecution was first of all drawn into speculation because Rouse himself volunteered the facts that he had a harem, that he found it expensive, and that he travelled about a lot. The police inquiries which naturally followed Rouse's statement proved that Rouse's boasts were true. At this point before the Police Court proceedings there was painstaking consideration by the Crown whether or not to proffer evidence as to his adulteries, and a positive decision was reached. Later there was a second consideration before the trial itself about using this mass of evidence at the Assizes, and then there was a change in the course adopted, for it was decided not to use it. This was unfortunate for the defence. After all the gravest charge but one known to our law was preferred against the accused and the effect of the pitiless publicity of our Police Courts is irrevocable and well known.

The initial idea clearly was to use this evidence about women to prove motive; also Mr D. G. Kennedy was called at the Police Court to prove that Rouse's car was insured as from 18 July for £1,000, payable in respect of the death of a passenger in the car, or of the owner if driving it at the time, which appears to go in the same direction, namely, the Crown's desire to prove the motive of Rouse's pecuniary position, needs, and financial possibilities. Moreover, in opening the case in the Police Court, Mr G. R. Paling, after an objection by Mr Finnemore, said:

'It is the duty of the prosecution to prove intent. The suggestion of the prosecution quite frankly is that Rouse intended to murder this unknown man and intended that the body should be mistaken for his own.'

The magistrates retired, and later announced that evidence would be admitted in view of the motive suggested.

According to another report, Mr Paling had previously also observed:

'It is not my business to prove motive, but this is the case of a man who was paying money to a number of women on orders of the Court which had been made against him, and only a few days before an increased burden was likely to be placed on his shoulders. He was a married man who was paying court to more than one woman other than his wife, and it might well be that he would have a wish to disappear and so unburden himself of liabilities pressing upon him. He had very little money, and was going to Leicester to get an advance from his firm. It is possible you will draw the inference from the facts that it would be no great inconvenience to him if that body had been mistaken for him, and it was thought he had been found burnt in the car.'

It is also obvious that if the Crown had adhered to these tactics at the trial, the prosecution would have been closely pinned down to this alleged pecuniary motive for the crime, and presumaby there would have had to be a decision whether to allege simply that Rouse would profit sufficiently by disappearing from his wife and his women friends, Campbell, Tucker, and Jenkins, or whether he was a member of some further conspiracy with some unnamed person to obtain the £1,000 insurance because of a death in the car.

If the jury had disbelieved this motive or these motives there would have been a weakening of one large part of the case. There would also be the risk, by no means negligible, of a judge ruling that the evidence of bigamous adultery was in fact inadmissible, which would naturally involve either a reshaping of the Crown case during its very progress, or else going into Court with alternative schemes in hand for the conduct of the case. Even had the evidence been ruled admissible the jury might have taken an adverse view as to the fairness of such tactics against a man accused of murder, and counsel as able as Mr Finnemore would undoubtedly and justifiably have made the most of such scruples. It is plain that there must have been consideration of all this as a matter of tactics, and that there must have been detailed consideration to see whether the case was not strong enough to obtain a conviction against Rouse merely on the combined circumstantial evidence, plus the direct evidence his conduct in itself had afforded.

The fact that Rouse had gone to Ivy Jenkins the day after the crime would have made the disappearance motive difficult to prove to a jury. The prisoner's own change of plan made the task of the prosecution extremely complicated. It is curious that both prosecution and defence had their difficulties increased by midway changes of plan!

The crime was a peculiarly revolting one, in which it was important to prosecute to a conviction, if the accused were indeed guilty. The Crown, therefore, wisely withdrew the evidence of arguable admissibility, and at the Assizes relied solely upon unquestionably admissible evidence. The jury's verdict probably demonstrated that the course could have been followed safely all along.

The 'harem' speech, given the circumstances in which Rouse uttered it, denoted neither motive for nor explanation of Rouse's night ride. He consistently offered one, and only one, explanation, namely, that he was going to Leicester to his firm to collect commission due to him, and this explanation was adopted by the Crown. His aimless bragging brought out clearly his incessant vanity and loquacity.

Difficulties such as the application of the principles of the *Makin* case are not confined to the case of Rouse. The question is really whether any method of public investigation at the preliminary stages of a crime, by a lay tribunal accompanied by full Press reports, is not often gravely unfair to an accused person, and whether the whole system is not ripe for improvement. Some would-be reformers have suggested the exclusion of the public from Police Court proceedings of this kind, others the exclusion of reports of such in the Press. A third school of thought advocates the adoption of either the French or the Scottish systems of preliminary inquiry whereby juries can hear nothing until the case is opened at the Assize Court. Our present system is certainly open to the comment that inadmissible evidence may be tendered before a lay tribunal, and can be reported sensationally all over the country, so that an unbiased jury may become practically unobtainable.

*

At the trial before Mr Justice Talbot the evidence against Rouse fell for the purpose of proof into three main divisions:

1. That the car was burnt by design, not accident.

2. That the position of the body was more consistent with a guilty course of dealing with the unknown passenger than an innocent course. (Parallel with this evidence about the body, evidence was also given that a mallet was found fourteen or fifteen feet in front of the car, with dirt dried upon it; and a few hairs were embedded in the dirt.)

3. That Rouse's whole course of conduct after the blaze was more consistent with guilt than with innocence.

The task of the defence, most ably but not successfully performed by Mr D. L. Finnemore and Mr A. P. Marshall, was to shake this evidence as far as possible in cross-examination, and to adduce whatever evidence they could from Rouse and certain other witnesses to controvert the testimony adduced by the prosecution.

The evidence relating to the burning and the body was in the main circumstantial; but upon the subsequent conduct of Rouse, direct. After the verdict there were about the usual number of public deprecations of the verdict because of circumstantial evidence; and the usual evidence was furnished by a section of the Press that the great cogency of circumstantial evidence is still misunderstood and underrated by the lay mind. It is impossible to go over the whole of the evidence in a trial whose verbatim transcript amounted to some quarter of a million words, but a single comparison of the two classes of evidence may be useful. For the circumstantial, the reader may be referred to the fusing of the windscreen frame in two places. Colonel Buckle deduced from that the existence of a continuous pressure of flame from a point beneath it, lasting for several minutes, such as could only be sustained from a continuous supply of petrol to feed it; and from that continuous supply and the fact that the petrol tap was found loose by one whole turn, he deduced that the petrol had been deliberately fed to the flame by leakage from the union at that point. The evidence adduced by the defence to the opposite effect is of great interest, but whichever theory the jury might choose to adopt would be in the last resort a matter of science, technique, or experience. The point was one which could be dealt with only in the light of science. Take in contrast to that the fact that Rouse lied about the destroyed car to every single person he met on the road between Hardingstone and London, in London, and on his journey to and from Wales. His explanation of the lies was that he did not want to be bothered about explaining a complicated matter to a lot of people. It will be obvious at once that it is easier to invent a further lie of that description than to invent a scientific hypothesis to account for the physical fact of a fused windscreen, a hypothesis which might have to stand the strain of experiment to see if it would hold good, whereas no one could experiment with Rouse's modes of thought.

In the Rouse case, circumstance after circumstance pointed in one direction – the guilt of the driver of the car. No one piece of evidence was conclusive by itself. A good many admitted of possible alternative explanations. No doubt the jury tried to add together all these possible alternatives to see if they could make the one broad alternative of innocence ring true. That the unknown chance passenger managed in the course of lighting a cigarette to set a car ablaze whilst its owner was many yards down the lane relieving himself; and that the latter went into too complete a panic to think of bringing assistance and fled from the scene; such was the broad alternative which the defence invited the jury to accept. But would all the circumstantial details fit into it? After a singularly fair summing-up, the jury found themselves unable to adopt it. The fact that a good two-thirds of the evidence was circumstantial in no way weakens the moral effect of their verdict. The occasions when relevant circumstantial evidence is unimpressive are those where it can have come about by accident, or been manufactured in order to divert suspicion from the guilty to the innocent.

In Hardingstone Lane there was no one associated with the crime but Rouse and the unknown victim. The victim could hardly have encompassed his own death in order to embarrass and incriminate Rouse. The dirt-stained mallet well illustrates the accidental type of irrelevant circumstantial evidence.

The evidence that the car was burnt by design and not by accident is worth careful study.

It may be useful to outline very simply the general plan of the petrol supply and control of the Morris Minor car of 1931. Petrol is supplied through the orifice near the middle rear of the bonnet into a petrol tank which lies behind the dash-board, when viewed from the position of the driver. This tank will hold about five gallons. When the petrol is turned on from the tank behind the dash, it flows by gravity through the petrol pipe and filters to the bottom of the float chamber of the carburettor which is at the near-side of the engine block, roughly about midway along it. Thence the petrol flows through another small filter and a small orifice into the carburettor float chamber. Within the float chamber there is a hollow metal float, through the centre of which a hollow needle passes vertically. The float chamber has a circular lid held on to it by a spring clip. If this clip is pushed off the lid, and the lid removed, the needle valve, the float, and also some balance weights will come away with it. The main petrol tap is just left of centre of the extreme front sloping floorboard, and it is at the top of the sloping board so that it can just be touched by a passenger's right boot-toe if he pushes his foot forward, somewhat upward and somewhat outward to his right; but the hand-brake lever and gear lever are so placed that it is hardly a comfortable or probable position in which to find the foot of a passenger whose leg is of normal length. The main petrol tap has a two-way flow, one being to the reserve supply in the tank, the other to the petrol in consumption.

It is hoped that this simple explanation will have made it clear that, assuming a 1931 Morris Minor's engine not to be running, and assuming also that some ill-disposed person wishes to set the car on fire deliberately, there are three places where direct contact may be made with the petrol in the car, not counting any loose cans carried. The first place to find naked petrol would be by unscrewing the cap on top of the tank at its normal inlet. The second would be to unscrew the nut around the main petrol tap under the dash-board, so that petrol would weep or leak from around the joint on to the floorboards and mat, and around the gearbox and through the junctions of the boards on to the road. The final way to make contact with naked petrol would be by removing the lid of the carburettor, and with it the needle and float. As the carburettor is under the near-side bonnet, it would be necessary to lift the bonnet before doing this, and then push aside the clip holding the lid on to the carburettor itself.

It is necessary to ignite petrol before it becomes mixed with air, if an explosion is to be avoided, as every user of a blow-lamp well knows; and a person applying a naked flame directly on to the petrol at any of these three places in a car would stand a good risk of at the least singeing his clothes or body. Now, a man wanting to set alight a human being in a car would not want to provoke merely an explosion, because the whole corpse, relatively uninjured, might be blown away, and the whole car be more disintegrated than burnt, perhaps hardly burnt at all. He would want a flaming fire of sustained consistency, lasting several minutes, in order to char beyond recognition a human body, which, after all, consists mainly of water, and is not an easy thing to destroy without a fire of enormous temperature.

In the confession published in the *Daily Sketch* of 11 March 1931, Rouse described how he first killed (or made unconscious) the unknown man by strangling him:

> Then I got out of the car, taking my attaché case, the can of petrol, and the mallet with me. I walked about ten yards in front of the car and opened the can, using the mallet to do so. I threw the mallet away and made a trail of petrol to the car. I took the mallet away with one purpose in view. Also I poured petrol over the man and loosened the petrol union joint and took the top off the carburettor. I put the petrol can in the back of the car.
>
> I ran to the beginning of the petrol trail and put a match to it. The flame rushed to the car which caught fire at once. Petrol was leaking from the bottom of the car. That was the petrol I had poured over the man and the petrol that was dripping from the union joint and carburettor.
>
> The fire was very quick and the whole thing was a mass of flames in a few seconds.

The prosecution had not the advantage of this confession – obviously substantially true – and their experts had to work backwards from the remains of the car and account for its condition at the first moment of being burnt. Nothing, of course, would remain of a trail of burnt petrol along a road, so that was one of the things it would be hardest to presuppose. Colonel Buckle, an eminent fire assessor called by the Crown, came amazingly near to many of the other causes of destruction in his evidence, concentrating most upon the petrol union joint, whose looseness he could not dissociate from deliberate manipulation. He was not quite so 'warm' – as children say in their games – about the carburettor during his own appearance in the witness-box, but he got on to it eventually, and in a most interesting way.

Throughout the examination-in-chief and cross-examination of Colonel Buckle, whenever the carburettor came up, Rouse stiffened the muscles of his leg into a marked condition of tension. It was not the evidence about the petrol union which worried him so much, but what might come out about his carburettor. Why? Presumably because petrol union joints may weep or leak accidently, but a carburettor top cannot come off accidently. Therefore, if Colonel Buckle stated that the carburettor top had been deliberately taken off and the jury accepted his opinion, Rouse's death-warrant would be signed.

In his evidence-in-chief Colonel Buckle gave a certain amount of evidence about this carburettor. He said it had fallen out of the engine block through the melting of the carburettor body, and had also fallen away from the petrol pipe union which went into the bottom of it. The metal in the carburettor had fused. It was composed of an aluminium alloy, and aluminium would fuse at 1,200°F. Colonel Buckle also thought that the petrol tank supplying it was nearly full when the fire started.

In cross-examination Colonel Buckle carried his theory about the carburettor somewhat further. He had found it surprising that the lower water joint near it was so completely burnt, but did not accept Mr Finnemore's theory that the water joint had been sprayed with petrol from the carburettor, as a result of the carburettor top being blown off. Colonel Buckle thought that the continuing fire, from the open carburettor end of the petrol pipe after the carburettor had more or less disintegrated and its float and valve had ceased to function as such, accounted for the burnt-out lower water joint. This, of course, could have been the case, but in fact was not, as Rouse very well knew, and the theory must have been comforting to him. The off-side front tyre was not burnt, which Colonel Buckle ascribed to the fact that the carburettor-fed fire was on the near-side of the engine; and also to the direction of the wind.

In re-examination, the Crown's expert further explained that he thought it very unlikely that the carburettor top would be blown off, because there was a very small space in the carburettor chamber that was also completely filled by a large float. There was one air leak through the needle, and another air leak to prevent getting an air lock, and those were quite enough to affect the pressure, so that one would not get the explosive condition inside the carburettor necessary to blow off its top. Still, on the assumption that the carburettor top had 'melted' and 'fallen' off, Colonel Buckle reasoned that there had been a fire in the space surrounding the carburettor from a *leakage* of petrol there.

The foregoing remarks are a mere summary of Colonel Buckle's evidence concerning the connexion of the carburet-tor with the fire, all of which merits close study. It will be remarked that he did not suggest for the Crown that the carburettor top might have been deliberately removed, but all the time that this highly capable and astute witness had been testifying for the Crown, he had been watching the reactions of Rouse to his evidence, and from the fact that the prisoner did not seem much disturbed by it, Colonel Buckle was led to think critically over his own chain of reasoning. After he had left the box the further possibility occurred to him that Rouse had deliberately removed the top.

For the benefit of anyone not familiar with this carburet-tor, it may be explained that if the top is taken off and petrol pours into it by gravity through the pipes leading from the tank, the float chamber, deprived of the float which has come away with the top, rapidly fills, overflows, and continues to overflow whilst the supply of petrol lasts.

Naturally, Colonel Buckle suggested this hypothesis to counsel for the Crown. If Rouse should go into the witness-box – as in fact he did – it could be put to him, quite fairly, in cross-examination, although it had not been produced by the Crown as part of its evidence for the prosecution. Although quite fair, it would come as an unpleasant surprise for those defending him, and would enormously increase their difficulties. This new point, the removal of the top by hand, was put to Rouse, and it was remarked by those present in Court how he blanched when the actual carburettor from his car was handed up to him.

This fragment of the case illustrates the 'cruel kindness of the law', in Mr Justice Talbot's phrase, in allowing an accused person to give evidence, as it has done since 1898. Rouse was here to be tested upon a deadly part of the evidence against him, by Norman Birkett, one of the greatest cross-examiners of the English bar.

On the whole, he did not come out of this too badly from the scientific point of view. If anything he showed too much knowledge, and must in fact have come rather near to indicating the exact course he took:

'The petrol from the carburettor could be lit from a person standing in the road?' – 'Yes, but you would get a flash in any case, and a very bad flash indeed with the amount of petrol in there [indicating the chamber].'

And in answer to a question: 'I have never lit a quantity of petrol. *When I light a blowlamp I always do it with a rag.*'

From the fact that Ivy Jenkins had noticed a shortening (as from a singe) of his eyebrows, Rouse may in fact have been slightly less competent than his confession detailed. But, substantially, his account was true, and has been accepted as such by the learned leader for the Crown.

Scientists are valued in law Courts – especially by jurors – not for their scientific detachment, but for their ability to throw weight on a particular side of the scale. To put it plainly, it is doubtful whether Rouse went to the gallows because a petrol union joint was found loose by one turn, or because a carburettor top was off. One single honest straightforward action on Rouse's part after the fire – an attempt to put out the flames or a sympathetic remark at the victim's fate – would have outweighed the effect of a battalion of experts on motor fires called on his side.

It is quite possible that Rouse deliberately arranged the body of his victim so that the petrol-soaked right foot and leg should project resting on the running-board in order to form the link between a trail of petrol on the road and the interior of the car. The left leg was doubled thigh against abdomen, as if the unconscious body was kneeling on its left side, and this would bring the knee just about where the petrol union joint would be leaking – in other words, Rouse probably arranged the body of the unconscious man so that the continuous drip from the petrol union joint should be feeding upon the left trouser leg, so as to maintain the most intense volume of flame. The face was placed downwards so that the uprising flame from the floor of the car would destroy its identity. Possibly the right arm was thrown over the seat so that the soaked right cuff should be near the petrol can at the rear; then if that can should catch alight before the arm had been reached from the flame on the body's left, the flame would extend up the right arm and shoulder to near the face.

Note the following questions and answers:

'I am suggesting to you that yours was the hand that fired that car?' – 'It was not.'

'And that at the time you fired that car your companion, picked up on the road, was unconscious?' – 'No.'

'And that he was unconscious by your hand?' – 'No.'

141

'And that he had been thrown in that unconscious position, face forward, into the car that you were to light?' – 'Most decidedly not. I should not throw a man. If I did a thing like that, I should not throw him face forwards. I should think where I put him, I imagine.'

'You would imagine what?' – 'Hardly that I would throw him down like nothing. That is absurd.'

'If you rendered him unconscious, would you have a delicacy about his posture?' – 'No, but I think if I had been going to do as you suggest I should do a little more than that.'

'Would you?' – 'I think I have a little more brains than that.'

Rouse's boastful loquacity is astounding and probably came near the truth. The Crown's theory was that the unconscious man was either thrown forward or had just pitched forward. The real truth is, I infer, that Rouse was too clever to do the main job by halves, and that he could in a grim and cynical way truthfully deny the Crown's theory. It did not go far enough. The victim was carefully arranged for total destruction. It is extremely difficult to think out any other disposition of the unconscious body which would achieve Rouse's desired result so certainly, given the type of car used here with its severely limited space.

*

The grim task Rouse had set himself he performed with the utmost competence. And there he came to a full stop. Quite probably what he had not reckoned upon was that the horrible sight of the burning car might revive memories of his war injuries, which were sustained at a moment when an aeroplane was collapsing in flames, indeed, whilst he was actually looking up at it. He had voluntarily run the risk of creating a display of horror similar to the one he remembered. That was one risk, how big or how little we cannot tell now. It may have been a cause of his subsequent foolishness, or it may have had nothing to do with it.

Not for one moment did any feeling of pity for the victim cross his mind. Such references as Rouse ever made afterwards to him – 'that scallywag' – were marked only by an entire lack of feeling, unless the final letter he is alleged to have sent to the Chief Constable of Norfolk just before the execution revealed anything different. That letter has not been made public.

Instead of showing humanity, even any pretence of it, Rouse callously alluded to the funeral pyre as 'a bonfire'. Before reporting the burning and possible death of his passenger to the police, in case the passenger had any relatives, Rouse went home to tell his wife not to worry. 'I did not want at the time to bring my wife into it, and I went home. The police were bound to be inquiring about my car, as the number and everything was plain, and I did not want her to be upset, and I said: "I will be back tomorrow."' He then thought it necessary to take a journey to Wales to see a girl who happened to be ill.

It is fascinating to speculate why Rouse could ever have hoped for a second that his extraordinary course of conduct would not be fatal to any theory supporting his innocence. True, he had been steeped in duplicity for years, and he must almost have forgotten how to face any facts other than the ones of his daily commercial transactions. The curious articles in the Press which were published as his, however authentic they may have been, all demonstrated an astonishing lack of human decency. 'There are two women in my life to whom I may go on my release, neither of them my wife', is a fair sample of the position to which his outlook on life had brought him.

Rouse had apparently abandoned the mental habit of facing facts as they exist. A considerable amount of material about him is extant, and it is remarkable that, if one compares his accounts of himself, one finds that he could not avoid meaningless lies about the most unnecessary matters. It was so natural for him to lie that he never gave a thought to the difficulties he might be creating for himself if his entire behaviour after the car burning were closely examined. He had lied to simple, gullible girls for years, and found it successful, but he never anticipated the moment when trained legal minds would sift his prevarications and inconsistent explanations. In spite of his pose as a man of the world, he was curiously simple upon two points which led to his undoing. One was that he did not allow for the possibility of any chance wayfarer coming along during or just after his extraordinary dealings with his car. The other was that he did not in any way foresee the great news value of a shrivelled corpse in a burnt-out automobile, with a hatless man disappearing from the scene, nor that every illustrated paper in England would publish a picture of it. It is known that Rouse expected merely a three or four-line paragraph on the discovery, and perhaps another short paragraph on the subsequent inquest. Just as the sudden appearance of Brown and Bailey wrecked his disappearance plot, so the publication in the *Daily Sketch* of the police interview with his wife on the morning of the 6 November ended his pose at the Jenkinses' home as the husband of Ivy Jenkins, and any possible intention to lie hid there, whilst the Northampton Police could innocently presume that the brace buckles, etc., were those he had been wearing; unless, indeed, Mrs Rouse should state that they were not his, and, according to her own account, as given in the Press, she did not go so far as that.

It is a very curious fact that Rouse seems never to have had any alternative scheme if anything went wrong with his extraordinary plan. He had been long weeks preparing it, and no doubt exists in any well-informed mind but that his victim had been marked down in advance and was well known to him. It may have been, as Ivy Jenkins has suggested, that the man was one of his blackmailers, or it may have been that he lured the man into his car by the promise of a job in the Midlands. At all events he did succeed in selecting an absolutely untraceable man.

Presumably it is one thing to perpetrate an efficient murder, and quite another, and infinitely harder, to anticipate every possible flaw in the attitude of innocence, and to devise a course of conduct afterwards which shall dominate the situation. After the murder every situation successively mastered Rouse, quite simply in the order of its appearance.

In the course of his prolonged inquiries, Mr J. C. Cannell of the *Daily Sketch* unearthed a most interesting and telling piece of evidence. On 1 November 1930 (four days before the crime), Rouse went to St Mary's Church at Islington, where he had bigamously married Helen Campbell in November 1924, in order to obtain a copy of the 'marriage' certificate. This document he could just as easily have obtained at Somerset House. Why then go to St Mary's? The clerk there, Mr Turner, might well remember him, and Rouse intended to trade on that fact and pose as his own brother, one possessing a startling fraternal resemblance.

To Mr Turner Rouse gave as his reason for wanting a marriage certificate the fact that his 'brother', A. A. Rouse, had just been burned to death in a terrible motor accident. A. A. Rouse's widow was then in London, and the applicant, as his brother, was carrying out the necessary legal and other formalities concerning his death on behalf of the widow. Such was his story.

In fact, the immediate purpose was to use the document to obtain Nellie Tucker's admission to the Maternity Hospital as his wife, and it was in fact so used.

I think the incident reveals rather more than my informant deduced from it. Not only does it go to show that Rouse was plotting the blazing car murder four days previously and associating himself with the idea of being a survivor, but it also illustrates Rouse's complete confusion of mind. He thought that he was creating a safeguard, namely, that Mr Turner would say, when and if he read of Rouse's car fire: 'Why, that is the very fire after which the brother of the dead man came to get the certificate for the widow!' And so, if he ever encountered A. A. Rouse in the flesh, he would think that it was merely the brother who called on 1 November. Rouse seems to have forgotten that a man in the fairly responsible position of Mr Turner would be far more likely to say: 'How very curious that Mr A. A. Rouse's brother should have come to me a few days *before* the fire and have described it as if it then lay in the *past*!' Mr Turner would then presumably have taken this appalling fact to the police, and the safeguard against any future identification would have become a death-trap.

Most of Rouse's answers in the witness-box revealed in one way or another an inability to reason, and a marked degree of confusion as to the order of events, and the importance of that order. To cite one remarkable illustration. At only the tenth question asked him, long before he could have become confused from tiredness, when Mr Marshall asked Rouse in examination-in-chief: 'In what year were you wounded?' this was the remarkable reply:

'A few months after I joined up. I joined on the 8 August, I think it was, and I was wounded on the 15 April. I believe it was February. 25 May, I think it was.' Most soldiers invalided from the war, who have drawn a pension from a given date, can state in under three guesses the date when they received the wound.

It may not be inappropriate to add a word of comment about the confession in this case. There were two documents, one of which, by Rouse himself, appeared in the *Daily Sketch* on 11 March, the day after the execution, the other, a letter from Mrs Rouse stating that he had confessed his guilt, appearing in the *News of the World* on the Sunday following.

The Home Office is determined not to publish murderers' confessions, and the newspapers are equally determined to publish them, if they are fortunate enough to get hold of them from a reliable source. The public wants them, and innocent prison officials are likely to have to continue to vindicate their innocence in such cases, as was triumphantly done on this occasion.

A debate was initiated on 29 April in the House of Lords by the Rt Hon. Lord Darling, in the course of which that eminent ex-judge read a letter from Lord Rothermere to the following effect upon the articles dealing with Rouse's life:

'I am very interested in the subject of the debate that you are initiating today, and I wish that my business engagements permitted me to attend. I gather you are to raise, among other questions, the increasing tendency of certain newspapers to publish, particularly in respect of murder cases, the life of the convicted person, notwithstanding that an appeal of the Court of Criminal Appeal may be pending. Speaking for myself – and I am sure my personal view will be shared by the proprietors of all reputable newspapers – I would welcome an authoritative ruling that matters to the detriment of the convicted person should not be published until the time for lodging an appeal has lapsed, or, if an appeal was lodged, then not until the appeal had been heard.'

That, remarked Lord Darling, was most valuable confirmation of the view that there was nothing to the detriment of reputable newspapers in omitting matters of the kind to which he had referred.

In the debate, Lord Darling expressed the view that the

exclusion of the public and Press from preliminary in-vestigations of sensational trials would be legal. But who is to decide what case is a sensational one?

The Lord Chancellor, in a temperate reply, expressed the view that although the articles Lord Darling complained of were regrettable and unfortunate, they had been con-sidered, and it was thought unlikely that the Court would hold that they constituted a contempt of Court. The Lord Chancellor commented on the value of the Press in the detection and prevention of crime, and gave a serious warn-ing that if articles such as those Lord Darling complained of should appear on any future occasion, they would be brought before the Court to ascertain whether a contempt had or had not been committed. He deplored the marketing of sensational stories in connexion with crime, and asked editors and proprietors to consider the undesirability of their publication.

At all events in this particular case among those who did *not* supply the confession which appeared in the *Daily Sketch* were the whole of the prison service connected with Rouse, and Messrs Darnell & Price, his solicitors. Rouse confessed his guilt to more than one person, but not at the same time.

After its publication Mrs Rouse naturally enough saw no point in maintaining her own loyalty to the guilty man, and published what she thought proper in the *News of the World*, although on 25 February she was alleged to have telephoned to Mrs Clynes (wife of the Home Secretary): 'I know he is innocent'; on 9 March there appeared in the *Daily Express* her alleged statement: 'I have been seeing him constantly, and he has consistently protested his innocence. I think it is unfair to him that such reports should be pub-lished'; whilst the *Daily Mail* of 12 March similarly alleged that it had 'excellent grounds for stating that Rouse died without making any statement whatever with regard to his guilt. His wife and lawyers give a categorical denial to the suggestion that he confessed.' The quite contradictory statements published by Mrs Rouse in the *News of the World* bore the date 7 March.

There were a few mild attempts in certain newspapers to controvert the *Daily Sketch* statement, in the light of inference and conjecture. Without being empowered to reveal my authority, I can state that the confession was authentic and substantially true, in spite of one or two comments which can be made on small points, and upon Rouse's obstinate statement that he did not know the identity of his victim.

It is notable that in the final letters Rouse sent to Helen Campbell, and to his little son, he not only made no protestation of innocence, but in the one to Miss Campbell he wrote: 'I expect I have been the most to blame.' Rouse also allowed Nellie Tucker to infer his acquiescence in the jury's verdict.

It is one cruel irony of the situation that the police have in their possession a statement based upon remarks by his little son which, if accurate, might have presented a plausible explanation of Rouse's crime. But the evidence of a child of five, however observant, intelligent, and tenacious, would hardly be presented by the Crown in a charge so serious as murder. A prevalent rumour that this child was examined by the jury, judge, and counsel in a private room is entirely baseless. To begin with, such a course would have rendered the whole trial absolutely invalid and afforded ample ground for quashing in the Court of Criminal Appeal.

What the jury did do was to conduct certain personal experiments with a Morris Minor car in a perfectly proper and legitimate way. These experiments removed their last doubts in the matter.

Just as the Crippen case was the first where wireless telegraphy brought about the arrest of a fugitive criminal, so the Rouse case was the first in which wireless telegraphy was used to summon a witness. Mr G. R. Paling needed the attendance of a certain Metropolitan police officer to prove certain distances. He was out on his beat at the time, and a wireless message was sent from Scotland Yard to a Flying Squad motor-car to find and take him to Northampton. Within two hours of Mr Paling's telephoned instructions he was in the witness-box, 65 miles away from London.

Another curious feature of this crime was that its inception *may* have been due, more or less, to a war spy story published in the *Evening Standard* in January 1929, or else that a work of fiction – 'The W Plan', by Mr Graham Seton – intelligently anticipated in certain ways what Mr Rouse did with his car and his passenger. The crime of Rouse was also paralleled by those of two German murderers, both of whom killed motor-car passengers to obtain insurance money. The first, Karl Erich Telzner, confessed to his crime and was executed at Regensburg, after expressing repentance, on 2 May 1931.

*

What might be described as a strong minority of the legal profession has expressed doubts upon this trial quite apart from the known and admitted guilt of Rouse. Their point of view boils down to the question: 'Was there sufficient evidence presented in Court to justify the verdict of the jury?'

To answer that question satisfactorily the reader would have to peruse the many pages of evidence given at the trial. Curious points emerge. The mallet of which so much was heard at the trial, and to which the Court of Criminal Appeal appeared to attach great importance, turned out to have no part in the crime, and all the fuss about the few hairs embedded in the dirt on it was an example of the wasted time and energy into which a piece of circumstantial evidence can occasionally mislead counsel. It did not weigh much with the eminent and astute judge who heard the case, but received some prominence in the judgement of the Court of Criminal Appeal.

Each juror will know what parts of the evidence most weighed in his own mind. All those present at the trial unite in declaring that Rouse hanged himself in the witness-box. The fact that the car debris indicated several practically simultaneous origins of fire guides one to think as one would in an approach to a case of arson. Most convincing of all was that the piece of cloth from the crotch or fly of the trousers, sheltered as it was by the peculiar bending (or constriction from rigor) of the human remains, was still damp from petrol after a fire which had melted metals near it, requiring heat to approximately 2,000°F. That shows more than a mere spraying – it was the effect of a deliberate drenching or soaking, and that should end the matter, even on a bare reading of the recorded evidence. If Rouse had led the life of Galahad, that petrol-soaked cloth was sufficient to condemn him, in the particular circumstances in which it survived such heat. Rouse's amply justified pride in his intelligent assessment of the best way to dispose a body in a car for burning would also have made one ponder things carefully. A skilled eye-witness has described Rouse's attitude throughout the part of the case dealing with the burning of the car as that of a person who knew what really had occurred, and who found the deductions of mere theorists slightly amusing. Rouse's apologists should recall that the whole point of a jury trial is a judgement of demeanour as well as of words, and that Press reports cannot give much more than the bare words, without their telling accompaniments of over-confidence or betraying reluctances. Rouse's verbosity must have been a severe trial to the devoted barristers defending him. It was a pure gift to counsel for the Crown. One wearies of counting the number of times

Rouse used the expressions, 'Honestly', 'Candidly', 'To be frank', etc. – all so unnecessary when a man is really being honest and remembering his oath.

Having read reams of his lucubrations about himself, plentifully besprinkled as they are with obvious and futile lies, it has become clearer and clearer to me that Rouse was a product of war – a war tragedy. Some people are blessed with a faculty for seeing war as a moral purifier. That is a very limited facet of the truth. The war did not purify Rouse – it markedly helped his moral ruin. It broke his morals, and I consider that his head wound broke his mental power and shattered his controls without lessening his conceit.

It was a curious coincidence in the life of Arthur Rouse that, when he was journeying home as a wounded soldier, he first regained consciousness while passing through a station where 'Bedford' was painted on the nameboard. It was in Bedford Jail that he was executed, fifteen years later.

Patrick Carraher
· 1938 AND 1946 ·

BY

GEORGE BLAKE

IN the case of Patrick Carraher it is important first of all to have a true picture of the social conditions in that part of Glasgow from which he came, the region around the historical Glasgow Cross; for these conditions played a large part in producing the kind of killer he was.

We are dealing here with a region in which quite decent people may regard four sleepers to a small room as luxury; in which the inhabitants of several households may have to share a common, and inefficient, privy on the landing; in which the privileges of dividend and cheque-book are wholly superseded, or anticipated, by begging, pilfering, peculation, assault, battery – a region in which, in fact, it is at once hard to bring up a family in decency and still harder for the family to resist the degrading social pressures about it.

The more murderous activities of this man Carraher were conducted in regions on or near the main axis running north-south through the most ancient part of the City of Glasgow from the neighbourhood of the venerable Cathedral steeply downhill past the site of the original College of Glasgow, then past the Tolbooth Steeple and the Cross; again down the Saltmarket and across the bridge over the Clyde into the district known as the Gorbals.

This section of a populous and crowded industrial city has acquired an adventitious notoriety, and on the whole, one fears, a vast number of people have been given an impression of a region of high, tottering, reeking tenements, peopled exclusively by characters in the *apache* class.

The real Gorbals is a much less picturesque district. Regarded as a bit of town-planning, most of it would be rather admired by contemporary architects. The streets run wide and straight, on the whole with plenty of light and air; the tenement buildings do not give the impression of utterly overwhelming narrow streets as they do elsewhere. An orderly colony of Jews of the poorer sort is respectably established in the area. It is, in fact, one of those old, solidly built, central districts of Glasgow in which the westward movement of the more prosperous created a vacuum, and into which, in turn, there flocked the poor and a good many of the shiftless.

Gross overcrowding was an inevitable result of this process. Good old houses were divided and then sub-divided, and the greed or ignorance of distant landlords did not fairly meet the needs of a rapidly expanding population. Patches of insanitary slum were created. And thus, inevitably, there appeared in the body of the historical Gorbals the canker of crime. The bad boys and girls of a clotted city, racked by racial and religious differences, tended to gravitate there, and they gave the place a bad name. It is merely necessary here to lay it down that the Gorbals is much less of a stew than many a corresponding area in other seaports; that the incidence of crime is indeed rather less seriously marked than in other districts of Glasgow alone; and that the vast majority of the local population strives at once to maintain decency in difficult conditions and to escape into more agreeable homes in wider fields. Town planning and redistribution of the population are gradually cleaning out this sordid area.

It was hereabouts, however, that a male child christened Patrick Carraher was born in 1906; and it is of importance that his father was a decent, respectable working man. We shall see later on how this Patrick Carraher developed into a hopeless recidivist. Our immediate concern is with the fact that, in the early hours of the morning of 14 August 1938, he first used a knife to kill a fellow-creature.

*

Gorbals Cross is the natural focus of the life of the district. This is quite a spacious circus, with a traffic island at its centre, and a crossing of importance in the city's transport scheme. North-south traffic by the Victoria Bridge across the Clyde is heavy throughout the working day, and it remains considerable until late at night, with trams, buses, taxicabs, and private cars carrying the considerable population of the suburbs on the south side home from work or recreation on the more sophisticated north side. It is inevitably the favourite meeting-place, and lounging-place, of many of the inhabitants of a grossly overcrowded area.

At 11.15 p.m. on the evening of Saturday 13 August 1938, an eighteen-year-old working girl, Margaret McKay McNicol, arrived at Gorbals Cross to meet by arrangement a nineteen-year-old window-cleaner called James Durie. The hour may seem late for such an assignation, but it would still be quite light in those northern latitudes and, as we shall see, the nocturnal habits of the Gorbals folk are apt to be eccentric. Margaret's first encounter at the rendezvous was with a man she knew as Paddy Carraher. He was alone, and she realized that he had been drinking. He explained that he wanted her to go and act as intermediary with a woman called Katie Morgan, a former lady-love with whom, it appears, he had had a misunderstanding.

Margaret McNicol declined. As she put it in Court subsequently: 'Well, the two of them fell out, and I didn't want anything to do with it.' In the light of the evidence we may imagine that this young girl, undoubtedly knowing Carraher's criminal record and alarmed by the truculence which had come upon him with drink, was chiefly concerned to get out of his company as quickly as possible. She even came to know that he had a knife on him, which suggests that Carraher, in his sour mood, boasted that he had a knife and would use it if necessary. Even at this early stage the reader should note the overtone of theatricality in all the more desperate utterances of Patrick Carraher.

Alarmed by this encounter – a girl of eighteen against a habitual criminal of thirty-two – Margaret McNicol looked about for succour and saw her boy friend, James Durie, not far away. She ran towards him. But Patrick Carraher followed her and grasped at her arm, tugging her away from Durie. Durie caught her by the other arm and tugged in his turn, the young woman helpless between them. In the issue of this formless brawl, the girl escaped from between Carraher and James Durie, and the two men came to grips.

This was a climax of some importance, as the High Court of Justiciary came to consider it later on. The burden of the evidence is that Carraher seized young Durie by the lapels of his jacket with his left hand and, with an open knife in his right, threatened him, the point of the knife menacingly aimed at the youth's midriff. This, if the evidence for the Crown is to be accepted, was assault in an advanced degree.

It was maintained by witness for the Crown that Carraher and Durie remained in this statuesque pose 'for five or ten minutes'; one wonders if even a couple of film stars could have so brilliantly 'held' such a powerful scene over such a length of time. The presiding judge at the consequent trial in the High Court, the late Lord Pitman, almost contemptuously dismissed this single issue in his charge to the jury. Considering the reported case after a lapse of many years, the layman may reasonably feel that the Crown – in the sense of mere tactics at least – put an excessive emphasis on this episode of technical assault and thus in fact, by dividing the interest, weakened the case of murder against Patrick Carraher.

However that may be, the two young people extricated

themselves from the grip of Paddy Carraher at Gorbals Cross and made towards Peggy McNicol's home in Eglinton Street, about a quarter of a mile away to the west. They would have done well to leave it at that, but it appears that, after a discussion in the close leading up to the girl's home, they decided to return to the Gorbals and continue the dispute. In fact, they made for 163 Hospital Street, where young Durie's older brother lived under the roof of his mother-in-law, Mrs Morgan. This John Dickson Durie, aged twenty-four, was then an unemployed labourer. Hearing his brother's tale of threatened assault with a naked knife, he rose, dressed, and went down with the others to Gorbals Cross. He thought it his business to see that his junior 'got a fair fight' – that is, against Carraher – but we may reasonably imagine that the Duries went out in force to maintain the family honour against a notorious troublemaker. This was a clan feud.

These Duries were not gangsters. The family record with the police was clean enough. They were rather of the class known in the *argot* of Glasgow as 'Neds' – that is, the rather shiftless lads who hang about street-corners and watch and wait: without much purpose, without definitely criminal intent, but with a wary eye for the main chance: the loungers on the edge of active society.

When these two Duries got down to Gorbals Cross at a late hour of the night, Paddy Carraher was not immediately in sight. They had, however, reinforced themselves. Peggy McNicol had gone home by this time and may now be forgotten; but with the Durie brothers at Gorbals Cross there were now Charles Morgan, aged sixteen, John Durie's brother-in-law, and Peter Howard, aged twenty-three, a shunter in good employment. By midnight or thereabouts the Durie clan thus felt itself no doubt ready for anything. In due course they spotted their man and went across to have it out with him.

According to the evidence of the Duries and their hench-
men their proposition to Carraher was that he should there
and then agree to a fair fight with bare fists with one or
other of the Durie brothers. To this Carraher would not
agree, and we may share the presiding judge's view that this
was only a prudent decision. He had taken a good deal of
drink, and he rightly feared that, according to the code he
knew so well, he might ultimately be beaten up by the
Durie faction. The argument became heated; Carraher was
heard to declare that if he had only two other men like
himself he would 'redd the corner' – that is, clear the place
of the Duries and their friends. It is one of the small curiosities of this case that Carraher is more than once reported as
speaking in good braid Scots instead of the debased *patois* of
his native city.

There then appeared upon the scene a strangely ill-fated
young man. This was a young regular soldier, James Sydney
Emden Shaw. Now, it is important that Shaw was little
known, or not known at all, to the Carraher-Durie group.
As they say, he butted into a private quarrel, perhaps with
some drink in him. He appears to have overheard Carraher's
brave boast of redding the corner, and he remarked to this
dangerous citizen that he 'spoke like an Englishman', or
words to that effect. This observation, which might gratify
a certain type of Scotsman, could not be construed by a man
of Carraher's stamp as anything but an insult. The ball of
controversy passed from the Duries to Shaw; and they
were all making such a noise that the policeman on the beat
intervened, telling them to 'take a walk' – the Glasgow
equivalent of the London Bobby's 'Move on, now'.

The party, Shaw still of the company, started to move
eastwards from Gorbals Cross along Ballater Street, and
Carraher and the soldier continued their highly personal
argument. They were 'throwing cracks' at each other; that
is, they were insulting each other, and there is no doubt

at all that Carraher was nagged and provoked by this intruder. Reaching the corner at Thistle Street, the older Durie wisely decided that he and his relatives should go home, and they started to move away. Peter Howard, however, lingered awhile on the edge of the pavement, Carraher and Shaw still wrangling in the roadway a few yards away. It appears that Shaw insisted on continuing his argument. The evidence here is somewhat obscure, but it is fairly clear that, as Howard was turning to follow the Duries, a scuffle on the roadway caused him to look back; whereupon he saw Shaw 'haudin' his neck' – that is, holding his neck – and pointing towards Gorbals Cross as if he looked for succour in that direction or hoped that Howard would seek it there. Carraher had meanwhile disappeared in the darkness. It was now after one o'clock of a Sabbath morning; and Paddy Carraher had the gift of swift disappearance from scenes of violence.

Peter Howard thus became, willingly or not, the leading actor in a tragedy. He was alone with a man bleeding to death from the jugular vein. A minor complication, of which the Defence ultimately made the best it could, was the appearance on the scene of a man in a light suit. From this passer-by Howard borrowed a handkerchief to stanch the flow of blood from Shaw's neck, and then he, also, disappeared into the shadows of the Gorbals. The episode seems to make a sinister convolution in the pattern of that night's events, but we may agree with the view of Lord Pitman that it was not a material point, and that any one of us, encountering such a situation late at night in a notoriously dangerous area, would readily produce a handkerchief and even more readily escape the scene of an affair so obviously involving police proceedings. The stranger in the light suit was in fact never traced.

In the meantime, Shaw had staggered to the corner of Thistle and Ballater Streets, where he collapsed. Then he rose again and, according to Howard, 'ran' westwards along Ballater Street towards Gorbals Cross: the trail of his blood clear to the detectives when they came to examine the scene. He passed under the viaduct that carries the railway lines across the Clyde into St Enoch Station and then, having covered some 150 yards, finally collapsed in front of a cinema. A policeman watching a shop nearby attended to him, and an ambulance duly arrived to carry him across the bridge and up the hill to the Royal Infirmary. He died as they were taking him to a ward. The detectives on the spot in the Gorbals arrested Peter Howard.

The bush telegraph of the slums works fast. Even at that small hour of a Sunday morning people were abroad, including one female witness who 'decided to go for a walk along with my daughter about 12.45 on the Sunday morning'. It very rapidly got about the Gorbals that a man had been killed, and that Howard had been arrested. A woman called Mary McCafferty, an unemployed domestic servant, aged twenty-two, went out with her friend Kate Docherty to see what was afoot, saw Shaw being put into the ambulance in Ballater Street about 1.40 a.m., and gathered that Peter Howard had been arrested. This Kate Docherty was friendly with Howard's older brother, Robert, and the two women went to inform him of what had happened. Their subsequent movements are of rather curious interest.

On their way towards the house in Portugal Street where Robert Howard was staying – that is, westwards and beyond Gorbals Cross – the girls encountered Carraher. He was in Norfolk Street, near its junction with Buchan Street. He spoke to them, no doubt anxious to have the latest news of what was happening, and he went with them to the close giving entry to 12 Portugal Street. There, while Kate Docherty ran upstairs, he waited with Mary McCafferty but said nothing. Shortly they were joined by Robert Howard and Kate Docherty, and all four then proceeded across the Albert Bridge towards the Central Police Station not very far away. On the way there, in the narrow and picturesque thoroughfare known as the Bridgegate, Carraher and the girl McCafferty lingered behind while Robert Howard and Kate Docherty went on to discover at the Police Office how matters stood with the former's young brother. An astonishing conversation ensued.

One is strongly tempted to believe that Carraher had in him that streak of vainglory which is apt to go with the temperament of the killer. With a good deal of drink in him, possibly with memories of American gangster films, he seems to have struck a pose as the strong-armed hero who has disposed of the enemy. At all events, he told this girl whom he hardly knew that it was he who had stabbed Shaw.

'I said, "What for?" and he says, "I was arguing with a fellow. He was very cheeky." I said, "How did you do it?" and he says, "With a knife," and he took a knife out of his pocket and showed me it. . . . It was like a pocket knife, a dark knife.'

When the girl protested that it would now go hard with Peter Howard, she had from Carraher the prompt and rather too romantic assurance:

'Oh, yes, they will let Peter Howard out because I will give myself up; I won't let him swing for it.'

One might think that he could then have walked into the Central and told the police what he had just told Mary McCafferty, but the heroics of Paddy Carraher were hardly so perdurable as all that. They were rejoined by Robert Howard and Kate Docherty, and started back again across the bridges to the Gorbals. On the way home Carraher walked next to the parapet, and Mary told the others what he had revealed to her as they waited in the Bridgegate. 'Show him your knife,' she urged, and Robert Howard asked: 'Have you got a knife?' To which Carraher blandly replied, 'No, I have not got a knife, but I possess a razor blade. It is still in the packet.'

When the detectives arrested Patrick Carraher later on that morning they found this razor blade on his person, apparently still in its original packet. They did not find a knife, for Carraher had in fact, unseen by his companions, slipped it over the parapet of the bridge.

The subsequent trial of Patrick Carraher for murder is of only limited interest as an exercise in detection. That it was he who stabbed James Shaw to death there is no doubt at all. He was in a drunken condition, and we may think that he believed his blow to be aimed at an older enemy than the young and foolish soldier who had crossed his path by accident. The proceedings in the High Court of Justiciary were remarkable only for the brief, not to say brusque, nature of Lord Pitman's charge to the jury. Some of the odd considerations we have reviewed – the matter of the knife over the parapet of the bridge, for instance – were not so much as mentioned by his lordship. If ever a jury was directed to reduce the capital charge to one of culpable homicide (*anglice* manslaughter) it was never more marked than in this case. It is only fair to observe that Lord Pitman had much in mind the factor of drink.

In the issue, the fifteen men and women who constitute a Scots jury in criminal causes returned the unanimous opinion that Patrick Carraher should be found not guilty of assault but, by the majority verdict allowable in Scottish procedure, that he was guilty of culpable homicide. Lord Pitman thereupon sentenced Paddy Carraher to penal servitude for three years.

During trial after trial over a period of at least fifteen years verdicts of culpable homicide were returned in murder trials, and it appeared that the new mixed juries were unwilling to pronounce sentence that would lead to execution by hanging. In one notorious case of a shooting near Perth the jury found the accused guilty of rape but the charge of murder not proven, whereas it seemed obvious to those of us who sat in Court throughout those days that the man in the dock could not have assaulted the young woman in the case if he had not first killed her sweetheart. The embarrassment of the judge in charge of the proceedings – the then Lord Justice Clerk, the late Lord Craigie Aitchison – was obvious as he hesitated to pronounce sentence.

It may very well be that the incalculable inclinations of the new mixed juries subtly affected the old Roman qualities of sternness with strict justice in Scottish criminal procedure, and the hypothesis was widely debated at the time, but we merely note the fact that social circumstances and the state of the public conscience had completely changed when, in March 1946, Paddy Carraher appeared before the High Court of Justiciary for the second and last time on a charge of murder committed on a November night in 1945.

*

After his release from prison Carraher appears to have deserted his native Gorbals and moved to the Townhead area of Glasgow, on the other side of the river. The attraction here was a woman, Sarah Bonnar; and her brother, Daniel Bonnar, a notoriously aggressive citizen, became Carraher's henchman in many an escapade. Given Bonnar's adventurous temperament and Carraher's prestige as one who had done time for killing his man, this couple were at once able to exert considerable influence in their district and class and almost certainly destined for more serious trouble with the police.

The Townhead of Glasgow is utterly unlike the Gorbals in layout and general character. It is an older settlement by far, and it scrambles over and along the slopes of those clay drumlins, or ridges, which are so marked a feature of the city. Historic and important buildings stand in or about it. The Cathedral, the ancient house known as Provand's Lordship, and the mass of the Royal Infirmary are at hand. Allan Glen's School, the Maternity Hospital, the Royal Technical College, and even the City Chambers lie within the grouping, which also includes more than one printing establishment of international repute. Many of the older domestic buildings are of great architectural interest and even charm, but too many of them have been overwhelmed by the internal pressures that are the curse of a great industrial city with narrow boundaries, and are now only festering slums. As distinct from the Gorbals of the broad level streets, the Townhead is rather a clotted congeries of twisting lanes and dark, steep streets lined with the tall, grey tenements of the industrial west. Public-houses abound. Much of this area has since been redeveloped.

In this favourable environment, then, in February 1943, Carraher and Bonnar enjoyed an orgy of violent misbehaviour. The Indictment at the subsequent trial charged Bonnar with breach of the peace, assault with a bottle, and kicking a woman; the items against Carraher included vicious assault on a man in a public-house in George Street – punching, kicking, and slashing with a razor to his severe injury – and then turning on three women with a razor, putting them in a state of bodily fear and alarm. For about a week between 9 and 17 February that year these two men seem to have been in an extreme state of offensive madness or drunkenness. The trial, however, which took place on 11 May, is of no criminological interest. The case was a plain one of lurid hooliganism. Carraher was sent back to jail for three years.

We may notice here how Carraher's development as a criminal was now not to be halted; it was proceeding only too rapidly. He had started in early youth with theft and assault and some clumsy burglaries; but once he had wielded a weapon and got away with it, as they say, and doubtless as he relied more and more on the stimulus of drink, arrogant brutality grew upon him. The circumstances of the period, moreover, favoured the lone wolf, the reckless enemy of society. Carraher was unfit for military service, having a weak chest and a bad stomach, and he luxuriated in an atmosphere in which easy money, deserters on the run from the Services, the black-out and psychological strain sombrely coloured low life in all British cities. Honest liquor was scarce, but the lack of it could be made up with cheap and potent wines, sometimes fortified with methylated spirit to form a cocktail of lethal strength. Shortages, controls, and the black market, along with the strain on depleted police forces, completed the picture of a gangster's paradise.

We should understand, however, that Carraher was not a gangster in the literal sense. He neither commanded nor belonged to a large and organized clan of law-breakers. He seemed to be content to operate with the able and enthusiastic assistance of his 'good-brother', that is, brother-in-law – though it was not actually in law in this case – Daniel Bonnar. Indeed, the sensitive student of the proceedings in both trials may get from the evidence an uncomfortable sense of Carraher's essential loneliness and will certainly note the fact that in neither of his two fatal assaults was he the original provoker of the conflict. In the Gorbals case he was threatened by the Duries and nagged by the intruding Shaw; in the second and final case we are now about to study, the trouble was undoubtedly stirred up mainly by Daniel Bonnar on one side and Duncan Revie on the other. Carraher's austere function was that of Lord High Executioner: the man with the knife or chisel, prepared at the critical moment to redd the corner. We may fairly see that he was doomed by his temperament and circumstances sooner or later to overstep the limit a fairly tolerant society imposes on its bad boys.

At the time of his last trial Carraher was nearly forty years of age, and his person was showing the signs of physical decline. His height was rather below the average, being 5 feet, 6½ inches; his sandy fair hair was thinning above the temples. His eyes were the most remarkable features of his appearance. Seen in profile they were heavily lidded, hooded, so that from the front they appeared to be mere slits. It was a sinister and apparently merciless visage, so far as these outward stigmata matter at all.

It was on the night of Friday, 23 November 1945, that Carraher committed his last crime. Again, there can be little room for doubt that it was he who struck the fatal blow, slashing with a chisel at a man's neck. At the same time, the evidence is highly confused, like the topographical nature of the scene; and counsel on both sides were dealing mainly with people of indifferent education and low mentality; some of them quite obviously concerned to make a show of their own innocence. It is perhaps legitimate here, however, greatly to simplify the story and take a short cut through the tangle of testimony, described by the Advocate-Depute as 'a mosaic of evidence which is rather like the disconnected pieces of a jigsaw puzzle'.

*

On the afternoon of this Friday in November 1945, then, three brothers of a family called Gordon left their father's house about 4.30 p.m. These were John, Joseph, and Edward Gordon: the first-named the oldest, with eighteen years' service as a regular soldier in the Seaforths and not long released from imprisonment in a German camp since Dunkirk.

These Gordons – there were eight brothers in the family – were not unknown to the police, but they had the reputation of being sufficiently clean fighters in the petty warfare of the poorer quarters, and they were not of the work-shy type. It is of pathetic interest that John, the old soldier, was notoriously the quietest of the family, and it is of at least a little importance that until the evening of his last day on earth he had remained indoors and had not touched drink. Apparently the Gordons had fallen foul of the Carraher–Bonnar faction, but whether for racial, denominational, or merely family reasons we do not know, and there is no evidence to show that they went looking for trouble in the first place.

Their first port of call was a house at 139 McAslin Street, in the Townhead, where there lived a sister married to one Duncan Revie – another of those somewhat unfortunate 'good-brothers' with a too highly developed sense of family loyalty. This Revie was a deserter from the Army and on the run, able to visit his wife with safety only on occasion. At 5 p.m. the four men went into the Coronation Bar next door to 139 McAslin Street, and there remained, drinking steadily, until about 7 p.m. They then decided to go down to the Rottenrow to Cameron's public-house (now vanished in a slum-clearance scheme) where John Gordon was well known, and there again they drank until near closing time, 9.30 p.m.

There is no indication that there was any sensible pause for food. Indeed, the two younger Gordons passed out under the influence of alcohol and may now, for our present purposes, be forgotten. In Cameron's pub the Gordons had meanwhile encountered a young man called John Keatings, another deserter, but from the Navy in this case. In evidence he admitted that when he, John Gordon, and Duncan Revie emerged from Cameron's pub they were all half-seas over.

In the meantime, probably unknown to the Gordons, Carraher and Bonnar had been drinking more or less steadily throughout the day and had passed the evening in Thomson's public-house, not far from Cameron's in the

Rottenrow. Apparently they left this place about 8.45 p.m.
and went down to Daniel Bonnar's house in the same street;
with them a little man called Thomas Connelly Watt, 'Wee
Watt', who was to prove the fatal witness against Carraher
in the subsequent trial. The Carraher–Bonnar party in the
house in the Rottenrow, womenfolk among them, then
decided that they should have a sing-song, and Bonnar
went out to secure supplies of drink and bring in such
kindred spirits as he might encounter on the way. He thus
made his way up the Rottenrow and opposite Cameron's
pub encountered the Gordon clan and its adherents either
emerging or just emerged from the premises.

We cannot now safely surmise whether or not this meeting was foreseen or planned; we do not know exactly why
the parties should have leapt so swiftly into violent action.
We do know that the handsome, fair-haired boy called
Keatings, of the Gordon faction, immediately roared his
intention to clear the street of lesser men, and that Bonnar
on his part doffed his jacket, laid it on the roadway, and
prepared for battle against this obvious enemy. It is safe
to surmise that both Keatings and Revie made for Bonnar,
and it is certain that Bonnar ran away, pursued by Keatings
at least. It is also fairly clear that there must have been an
exchange of blows. After a brief chase, however, the affair
fizzled out. Keatings, in a tolerably advanced state of drink,
disappeared from the scene and had no further part in the
affair. But he had done his bit to set the heather on fire.

Bonnar now retired to the house of a sister in College
Street, his blood up, and there borrowed (a) a hatchet and
(b) a woman's costume jacket to replace his own jacket
that had been left on the roadway opposite Cameron's pub.
Thus strangely attired and heavily armed he returned to the
fray, and on the way he met Carraher and 'Wee Watt'
near Weaver Street. They had been warned that the good-
brother was in trouble with the Gordons and they had

come out to support their friend. A Mrs Helen Josephine Colquhoun, wife of a soldier and a temporary postwoman in her own right, had been cleaning her windows, even at 9.30 p.m., and had seen Bonnar chased along the Rottenrow by Keatings. She had thus conceived it her neighbourly duty to go down to Sarah Bonnar's house in Tarbet Street and tell her that her brother was in a fair way to be seriously assaulted.

The details of the next phase of the operations will probably remain forever shadowy. It is merely a simplification of complicated and rather suspect testimony to say that, after the first encounter with Bonnar and the disappearance of Keatings, John Gordon and Duncan Revie went up from the Rottenrow into McAslin Street; and that, in the meantime, Carraher and Bonnar, with 'Wee Watt' in attendance for a while at least, executed a flanking movement through the dark, dull streets and came upon their enemies again near the intersection of McAslin and Taylor Streets.

Whether 'Wee Watt' was actually present or not does not matter now. It is certain that the factions then clashed. Revie went for Bonnar, and again Bonnar executed a rapid retreat downhill, pursued by Revie. It seems equally certain that John Gordon, no doubt swaying pretty hopelessly on the edge of the pavement, was pounced upon by Paddy Carraher. When next seen by a fellow-creature he had collapsed on the pavement and was bleeding copiously from a wound at the back of the neck.

Of this tragic scuffle late at night and at an ill-lit corner there were, however, four good witnesses, if from various distances. Two more than middle-aged tradesmen, both respectable painters, had been chatting at the corner nearby. They did not claim to have heard sounds of scuffling, but they did hear voices raised in sundry incitements to violence, and they saw certain things happening. From some sixty yards away two much younger men heard the commotion and had seen very much what the painters had seen.

None of these witnesses could identify any of the men taking part in the brawl, and they differed as to the number involved: an agreeable symptom of their honesty. They all agreed as to the shouting of the men fighting, and they all saw two, or three, men running away down McAslin Street, one (or two) apparently in pursuit of another. They all saw still another figure advancing and 'punching' the man who stood on the pavement's edge. They all agreed that, when they went to the aid of the man who had been seemingly 'punched', he was bleeding copiously from a wound at the back of the neck. This man was John Gordon.

The evidence becomes slightly confused again at this point, but it is perfectly clear that some of these four witnesses started to help John Gordon to the Royal Infirmary, not far away. An unidentified sailor came to their assistance. The two ageing painters prudently disappeared from the scene. One of the two remaining witnesses – a young private in the Royal Marines called Neil Campbell – hastened to call a taxi to take the wounded man to hospital. The latter collapsed at the junction of Stanhope Street with McAslin Street as they were helping him along, but he appears to have been persuaded to his feet again. And then, an extremely odd incident, Duncan Revie reappeared, took the wounded person of his brother-in-law on his shoulder, and carried him up to the second-floor landing of the close at 139 McAslin Street, even though he must have seen that Gordon was rapidly bleeding to death.

We may surmise that Revie was in a state of high excitement and even apprehension; no doubt he had in his confused mind the notion of getting his good-brother into the care and protection of his own clan. Marine Campbell, however, had meanwhile found a taxi-cab, and Gordon was rushed to the Royal Infirmary. There he died exactly a minute after the doctor on duty at the gatehouse had made a superficial examination of his injuries.

Approximate silence then fell on the Townhead of Glasgow. From the evidence it is clear, however, that the affair had made a stir, and that sundry parties concerned continued to hang about, awaiting developments, their sombre curiosities not unnaturally aroused. One of the most important of these as a fatal witness against Carraher was a tall, twenty-seven-year-old part-owner and driver of a taxi-cab, John Douglas Stewart.

It was he who had been with Marine Campbell at the corner not far from the scene of the assault. He had helped to get John Gordon along McAslin Street towards the Royal Infirmary. Whatever he had done with himself thereafter, at about 11.30 p.m. that night, in either Cathedral Street or its brief extension into Stirling Road, he encountered an acquaintance, George Ross Elliott, nicknamed 'Gasser' Elliott, apparently on account of his conversational proclivities. These two discussed what had happened, and they set off together, near midnight, to look for Daniel Bonnar, whose name was being freely mentioned as the author of the crime. It is only fair to say that Stewart knew little of the parties concerned and proved to be an intelligent and useful witness.

Elliott and Stewart thus went first to Bonnar's house in the Rottenrow. There was nobody there, and they proceeded to Sarah Bonnar's home at 14 Tarbet Street, where after some hesitation they were admitted by Bonnar. Men and women were assembled in the kitchen, Carraher among them, and we get from the evidence a strong impression of excitement, now heightened by Stewart's intimation that Gordon was dead. It is of importance that Stewart had never seen Carraher before. Ultimately, after a great deal of talk backwards and forwards, Carraher invited Stewart into another room. The report then reads:

'Do you remember one of the people in the house coming up to you and asking you to speak apart?' – 'Yes, the accused asked me who I was, and I told him it did not matter. He said "Where do you come from?" and I said, "Over the road."'

'Where did this conversation between you and the accused take place?' – 'In the kitchen. That was when he asked me, and he said, "Well, come here a minute," and he took me through a door into another room. . . .'

'What happened when you and the accused were in this other room?' – 'He told me that he was having a cup of tea in the house when someone came and told him Bonnar was in trouble in the Rottenrow, and he went out and met Bonnar, and the two of them went to a close in McAslin Street, but they didn't see anyone there and they went to the corner of Taylor Street and met the two fellows and the fight started. . . .'

'Try and recollect the actual words the accused used?' – 'He just said, "I gave one of them a jag and ran away when the fight started."'

Bonnar was later to testify in the same sense, but this was an astonishing statement to make to a stranger. Carraher seems to have had a purpose, however, for when they returned to the kitchen and Stewart showed a clear desire to escape from this alarming situation, Carraher slipped something into his hand, saying, 'Chip that away'. When Stewart was outside again with 'Gasser' Elliott he found in his hand the short, sharp blade and the wooden handle of a woodcarver's chisel.

It seems strange that Stewart did not march straight to the Central Police Station with this incriminating object, but we can make allowance for the excitement and alarm of the situation and for the presence of Elliott. Instead, they dropped the blade down a stank in the High Street – that is, through the grating over a gutter drain – and the handle down another some yards away, having to use force to get the bulbous wooden part between the bars. These objects were recovered by the police within a few days.

This was not such absolute proof of Carraher's guilt as a judge and jury would accept out of hand, but the odds were narrowing.

Elliott followed Stewart in the witness-box and added some useful detail. He had seen Carraher draw the weapon from his hip pocket and break it into its two parts before handing it to Stewart. He had seen the accused wipe it with a dishcloth, but had not noticed any stain resulting. He had seen Bonnar take off a bloodstained shirt but understood that this was the result of one of his scraps with the Gordon faction; and Bonnar testified that he had been struck on the side of the head. Elliott had observed that Bonnar was excited, Carraher calm.

With regard to the nature of the wound of which John Gordon died there was some interesting testimony from the medical witnesses. It ran *upwards* from near the back of the neck to penetrate the cerebral canal; and at the post-mortem examination it measured four inches by the probe, whereas the effective length of the carver's tool was only about $2\frac{1}{2}$ inches. The defence naturally sought to make the best of this disparity, but expert evidence for the Crown was able to show that (a) in the case of a blow delivered with force the surface tissues would 'give' considerably under the impact, and (b) that there would ensue a considerable swelling or infiltration of the soft tissues by subsequent bleeding. Professor Allison's citation of the swelling seen in a case of mumps provided a convincing illustration. So far as the upward track of the wound is concerned, it is not difficult to see that Gordon probably crouched head downwards to receive it, and that the assailant would be pulling a clenched fist towards himself at the lowest point of his stroke. The discovery of a cut on the ring finger of Gordon's right hand would surely indicate the involuntary raising of a hand to protect the vulnerable neck.

We may now return for a moment to the scene of the

scuffle at the corner of McAslin and Taylor Streets, if only in order to clear away some of the confusion surrounding the figure of Carraher in that setting. Was it certainly he who was seen to 'punch' Gordon in the view of the four detached witnesses?

Whatever the motives of those pugnacious 'good-brothers' Revie and Bonnar, they exculpated each other in their separate testimonies. Revie was quite certain that he chased Bonnar down the street, Bonnar that he retreated before Revie, both leaving Gordon alone of his faction on the pavement; and Revie swore that he had seen Carraher menacing John Gordon. Was 'Wee Watt' among those present? Bonnar insisted that he was, but the defence, though naturally concerned to imply the possibility, made no overt suggestion that he struck the fatal blow or that he had ever been in possession of a weapon.

If Carraher was not thus indicated as the assailant beyond any reasonable doubt it was left to 'Wee Watt' to provide the most damning circumstantial evidence.

One is tempted to pity Carraher for the scurvy service he received in the witness-box from those who had been his cronies and sycophants. As will be seen from his evidence, Thomas Connelly Watt, aged forty-seven, was at some pains to tell the whole truth as he knew it of the happenings of that night, and it should be observed that the keenest cross-examination could not break his story. Briefly it went thus:

Watt was with Carraher and Bonnar in the latter's house when, after the session in Thomson's pub, it was proposed they should have a sing-song and Bonnar went out to bring in a friend. Then the news had come in that Bonnar was being chased by the young sailor, Keatings, and Carraher and Watt had emerged to see what was happening. Then, according to Watt, the carver's tool was in Carraher's breast pocket, the sharp edge showing. 'He showed the blade from the top pocket,' said Watt. He ran his thumb across the cutting edge, and said to Watt, 'This is the very tool for them.'

If that was not enough, Carraher was to make in Watt's presence another candid confession of his guilt. This was when, the fighting over but before the arrival of Stewart and Elliott with the news of Gordon's death, the Carraher–Bonnar faction had reassembled in Daniel Bonnar's house in the first place. In this instance Carraher demonstrated how he had dealt with his enemy, dancing on tip-toe like a boxer, the right hand swinging backward and forward, and then the upraised arm and the vicious stroke downwards. 'He said he did not know whether he had got him down the side of the face or shoulder,' Watt testified.

The presiding Judge, Lord Russell, invited Watt to demonstrate these sinister movements, and those who were present in Court declared that 'Wee Watt's' vivid panto-mime of a vicious assault was far and away the most telling evidence the Crown produced during the three days' hear-ing of the case. They also report that, throughout the proceedings, Carraher bore himself coldly and glumly, like one who knows his doom is sealed, his narrow eyes hooded and never a glance towards one of his enemies or his former friends in the witness-box.

In the early morning of 24 November 1945, the Glasgow C.I.D. acted swiftly and arrested several of the principal participants in the brawl. Most of these were ultimately con-victed for breach of the peace, while Carraher alone faced the charge of murder. The trial took place on Thursday, Friday, and Saturday, 28 February and 1 and 2 March 1946. After the judge's careful charge it took the jury only twenty minutes to return a unanimous verdict of guilty. On 6 April 1946, after an unsuccessful Appeal, Patrick Carraher was hanged in Barlinnie Prison, Glasgow.

*

The case for the defence rested entirely on medical evidence, provided by two experts who presented the view that Carraher's was a psychopathic personality and suggested that the then rather newfangled doctrine of diminished responsibility should apply to his violent actions.

In his able speech for the defence Mr G. R. Philip, K.C., covered a great deal of ground, perhaps attempting, one may think, to cover too much. He made his plea for Carraher under three distinct heads.

In the first place, quite legitimately, learned counsel set out to discredit certain leading witnesses for the Crown, notably Revie, Bonnar, and Watt, and so to handle the confusing evidence as to suggest that someone other than Carraher, perhaps Bonnar, had struck Gordon; and in this passage naturally he emphasized the apparent disparity between the length of the carver's chisel and the length of the wound in post-mortem conditions. With the evidence on paper before us we may feel that these attempts were hopeless in the light of Stewart's detached testimony, and the evidence of the doctors for the Crown.

Mr Philip, then, momentarily accepting the hypothesis that his client had been the killer, not altogether unreasonably argued that, considering the confusion of events and the amount of provocation supplied by Revie at least, this was no case of deliberate intention to kill. All the lurid events of the evening had been working up to a clash in which hard blows would inevitably be exchanged. This, argued learned counsel, justified the view that Carraher's crime, if any, was rather in the nature of technical homicide than in that of murder.

Finally, and most onerously, he rested his plea on the issue of diminished responsibility spoken to by his three expert witnesses as against the evidence and the firm opinion of Dr Scott, the prison doctor. Here is an issue which, in view of the latterday campaign for the abolition of the death penalty, involves the whole structure of our penal system and the public attitude towards crime. Judge and jury were invited in this case to consider a measurement or assessment of human responsibility that must at any time be infinitely more difficult to make with certainty than the sufficiently onerous assessment of a degree of lunacy. It will be noted that none of these experts for the defence would have certified Patrick Carraher insane. His was a psychopathic condition; he had alcoholic tendencies in a marked degree, and therefore his general sense of social responsibility was so far impaired that he could not properly appreciate the consequences of his acts. He knew the difference between right and wrong – but the distinction somehow did not apply to himself.

Another age would have called this sheer egoism, and the layman may wonder if the generalization could not be applied to the vast majority of criminals. However that may be, the student should address himself to Dr McNiven's able exposition of the theory, particularly to the passages at the end of his testimony when, in re-examination by Mr Philip, he uttered some easily understandable definitions. Also to be noted is his view that, so far from being willing to define a general line of demarcation in such cases, he thought each case should be taken on its own merits. There was again Dr Blyth's somewhat alarming estimate that psychopathic conditions, just below the ceiling of certifiable insanity, affect two per cent of the population. Finally, there came Lord Russell's admirably complete and fair presentation of these issues to the jury, unanimously approved by the Appeal Court.

The defence invoked a legend of the traditional stepmother who put Carraher from the house at an early age, but this romantic interpolation must be qualified in the light of information that was not produced in Court. Paddy's dismissal from his father's house was the deliberate act of both parents, sickened and saddened by his incorrigibility. The list of his convictions from first to last is a lengthy chronicle of misdemeanour and imprisonment over some twenty years, so that he spent much more of the second half of his life in prison than out of it, with a spell of Borstal intervening. His father was an anxious listener in Court at the first trial for murder in 1938, but he made no appearance at the second and last.

There were also introduced into the proceedings certain vague suggestions of a persecution mania. The medical witnesses for the defence found Carraher harbouring a general grievance against the Law and the police, surely a familiar attitude among inveterate criminals. There was also the account of his occasional trick of looking into cupboards for men who were not there. As for the man's grievance against people 'piping' him in public-houses, anyone who has visited an East End pub knows the sodden wreck with a chip on his shoulder, to whom even an accidental look is an insult to be wiped out only by abuse or assault.

On the whole, it seems fairly clear that if the defence had rested wholly on the plea of chronic alcoholism in Carraher's case it might have helped him more than the somewhat experimental plea of diminished responsibility, advanced by two doctors who had not seen a great deal of him, and then only when the strict regimen of Barlinnie had allowed the drink to work out of his system.

The fatal brawl was undoubtedly provoked and inflamed by drink. A telling fragment of Sarah Bonnar's evidence was to the effect that Carraher could rarely face a proper meal. A close student of this case, highly qualified to judge these matters, has privately declared that men like Carraher probably drank rather less in the average day than many a wealthier and better-fed man of invulnerable respectability, but that the absence of substantial food to absorb and offset the effects of alcohol would tend to enclose such men with, as it were, a glasshouse of morose illusion, into which a stranger might break only at the risk of violent assault.

The social problem symbolized by the public-house in such clotted cities as Glasgow is a heart-breaking one indeed. In Glasgow in particular it is complicated by the fact that strong pressure by the extreme elements of the temperance movement, working over a long period of years and with influence on the licensing Bench, has tended to turn the average public-house in the poorer districts of the city into a species of penal establishment. Even the most harmless games, such as dominoes and darts, are not permitted, and the police are forced by superior instruction to exercise the strictest supervision of licensed premises, while any effort by a progressive licensee to improve his premises to the standards prevailing in, say, England does not have the encouragement of the magistrates.

Even so, the public-house in those overcrowded districts of central Glasgow is an important part of the social structure. Given grossly overcrowded conditions of housing, the menfolk at least are simply driven out of their mean, stinking, insanitary, and often bug-ridden homes. If it is not to be wholly a matter of hanging about the street corner with the other 'Neds', it must be the pub, especially in a notoriously wet climate. It would be a vicious irony to suggest that the Glasgow working man's pub is his club. It is occasionally so, let us admit, but on the whole it is simply a refuge from the degradation of so many homes, from the meanness of the environment.

A terrible case has developed against those who have governed Glasgow during the past century. Throughout the long period of industrial expansion so little foresight went to the problems bound to arise when peoples of half a dozen races scrambled for work in an expanding city, when land-owners and property-owners allowed dwellings and their

179

sites to be divided and sub-divided, to be built over again and again, producing warrens in which the impoverished detritus of the old industrial order multiplied and festered. The maintenance of decency in such conditions is much more than a simple social duty; it is a feat. Fortunately much has already been planned and done to clear the city of its worst slum areas, but the leeway to be made up is still an immense problem.

Much has been made of gang warfare in Glasgow, and of those bands of pugnacious youths who, under fancy names, banded to fight each other on such pretexts as the old Billy and Danny rivalry, Protestants against Catholics. The pretexts are meaningless. The emergence of a Scoto-Irish breed, mainly huddled in the most degraded areas, did indeed complicate the pattern, but its basis was the essentially Scottish one of the clan system. Strong and violent youth unconsciously organized itself in groups in order, one had almost said, to fight its way out of sombre monotony. Theirs was only a special and unpleasant expression of the motive that bids millions rather more fortunately placed to sublimate their sense of frustration in blind loyalty to this or that football team. It is of touching interest that a sympathetic police official of one of the eastern divisions of Glasgow could, by 1942, show from his careful records that most of his notoriously bad boys were by then serving, if they had not already fallen, in North Africa or in the various Commando raids on the European coasts. So badly did they need a way of escape from the home environment and from the doldrums of unemployment that so terribly afflicted the industrial regions of Scotland during most years of the third decade of the twentieth century!

It has been suggested here that Paddy Carraher was not cut out to be a good gangster. His morose and individualistic temperament fated him to operate within small groups and usually as the Big Man with a somewhat theatrical fondness for the part of the decisive killer: the vicious egoist *in excelsis*. It has not been suggested, despite modern psychological science, that he was anything but a rat, acute and resourceful within his limitations. It has not been claimed that he was ever involved in a case of subtle interest to students of crime. One would like to think, however, that this account of his killings, trials, and subsequent punishment may assist in moving the public conscience and the authorities towards a more urgent sense of the appalling problems of housing and reconstruction, and of the gravity of the human problems arising out of bad environment, that still face many another British community besides Glasgow.

John Thomas Straffen

· 1952 ·

BY

LETITIA FAIRFIELD *and* ERIC P. FULLBROOK

In the period of ten months between 10 July 1951 and 29 April 1952, there occurred in the south of England a terrible series of murders, the victims being four little girls. The first to die was Christine Butcher of Windsor; four days later, on 15 July, five-year-old Brenda Goddard was strangled in a wood in Bath, and on 8 August Cicely Batstone was killed, also by manual strangulation, in a field on the outskirts of that city. Immediately after this last murder a man named John Thomas Straffen was arrested and charged with the killing of the children Goddard and Batstone; having been found insane on arraignment, he was committed to Broadmoor 'until His Majesty's pleasure be known'. Six months later, on 29 April 1952, Straffen escaped and within a few hours murdered the fourth child, Linda Bowyer.

The murder of children has always excited particular horror in civilized communities, not only because of the pathos of a life prematurely cut short, but because of the circumstances usually associated with such events. Sometimes the murder has been only the culmination of a long history of cruelty and neglect; sometimes it has been the impulsive act of a lunatic. More commonly there is reason to believe that a sexual pervert has been at work and the killing (usually effected by smothering or strangling) was evidently done either to stop outcries or from fear of recognition. It does not follow that, because there is no evidence of interference, the murderer was not impelled by a sexual motive. He might have been alarmed before he could complete his original purpose, or the killing might have been a substitute for the sexual act in some abnormally constituted person. Straffen had not interfered with any of his victims (unlike the still unknown murderer of Christine Butcher) and his declared motive was grotesquely inadequate by ordinary reasoning. 'I did it to spite the police,' he has said on many occasions. Fantastic as it may seem, this appears to be the truth, if not the whole truth. To get nearer the heart of the mystery one must follow the prosaic life-story of a certified mental defective for the first twenty-one years of his life.

*

The lad who came to such dreadful eminence in the history of crime was the third of the six children of John Straffen, formerly a regular soldier. A boy and girl were older than John, and three girls younger. John was born on 27 February 1930, at Borden Camp, Hampshire, where his father was then stationed, and when he was two the family went with the regiment to India for six years. According to his mother, they all thoroughly enjoyed this experience. Although tests by the electro-encephalograph were said to suggest an early meningitis, Mrs Straffen was emphatic that during his early years John had no serious illness, no sunstroke, he was never separated from her to go to hospital or for any other reason, and indeed was an ordinary healthy little boy, except that he spoke late and developed a speech defect which he retained for many years. He seems always to have been slow in learning.

In March 1938 the family returned from India and the father took his discharge after nineteen and a half years' service. Apparently John began to give trouble very soon after they arrived in Bath, for by October 1938 he had been referred to a Child Guidance Clinic for pilfering and truancy. A few months later (June 1939) he was brought before the Juvenile Court, after several police warnings, for stealing a purse from a little girl, and was put on two years' probation. But the Probation Officer, Mr Sidney Harding, to whose care John was committed, found his task an impossible one. He had a vast experience of naughty boys, but here was something different, a real 'problem child'. He found the boy so defective in intelligence that he was unable to understand what probation meant, he was learning nothing at school, his conduct was going from bad to worse, and he had no ordinary understanding of right and wrong. Home cooperation with the Probation Officer's efforts was poor, for the unfortunate Mrs Straffen, who admittedly had more than her fair share of the family burdens to carry, was overwhelmed by the care of six young children in crowded lodgings. Recognizing that in this sort of situation probation can be worse than useless, Mr Harding took John to a psychiatrist and on his doctor's recommendation the difficult youngster was certified as a mental defective under the Education Act of 1921.

As the diagnosis of mental defectiveness was to play such an important part in the boy's later life, it may be helpful to remind the reader at this point of the legal implications of this much-misunderstood term. By statute it is defined as

a condition of arrested or incomplete development of mind existing before the age of eighteen years, whether arising from inherent causes or induced by disease or injury.

Defectives have often been called 'permanent children': they may be physically quite normal but are afflicted by a sort of mental dwarfism which keeps them always mentally smaller than those of their own age. There is a definite distinction between mental defectives, who have never had normal intelligence, and the insane, who have once had it but lost it by mental disease; it follows that mental defectives are by definition *not* insane.

Under the Mental Deficiency Act of 1927, defectives were divided into four classes: idiots, imbeciles, moral defectives, and the feeble-minded. With three of these we need not trouble, for young Straffen clearly fell into the category of the feeble-minded, who are defined as follows:

Persons in whose case there exists mental defectiveness which, though not amounting to imbecility, is yet so pronounced that they require care, supervision, and control for their own protection or for the protection of others or, in the case of children, that they appear to be permanently incapable by reason of such defectiveness of receiving proper benefit from the instruction in ordinary schools.

Children of school age were before 1944 normally certified as M.D. under a section of the Education Act 1921. They are now called 'educationally sub-normal'.

How does one distinguish these higher-grade defectives from the merely dull and backward children and adults? It is never easy and would be quite impossible without the yardstick of the intelligence tests which, with all their faults, do enable a rough line to be drawn. Perhaps one should add that intelligence tests do not represent what psychologists think children of certain ages *ought* to know, but what many thousands of tests on normal children have shown that they *do* know. The tests must of course be applied with sympathy and common sense; the confidence of the child must be won and full allowance made for lack of schooling, poor physical health, emotional disturbance, abnormal circumstances in home life, etc. But these are commonplace precautions with which the psychologists at the Bath Clinic and the other institutions where Straffen was examined were perfectly familiar.

The report of 1940, when he was ten years old, states

that his Intelligence Quotient was 58 and his mental age six. He could read his letters and two-letter words and could only add in units. His manner was

cheerful and friendly and he seemed well able to care for and protect himself, his chief defect appears to be lack of concentration – no harmful characteristics.

His teacher had reported him as amenable, affectionate, not spiteful, but the boy had told a psychiatrist that he hated her and the school, 'as he was sometimes punished'. At the instance of the Juvenile Court, John was sent by the Bath local authority to a residential school for defective children in June 1940. Although the Straffens were Protestants, a Catholic school was selected as vacancies elsewhere were hard to obtain.

The public is greatly concerned nowadays by the possible injury done to children by confinement in an institution, but it has to be admitted that John Straffen might have fared much worse. During his two years at St Joseph's, Sambourne, he was under the care of Sisters highly trained in the needs of retarded children and advised by educational psychologists and psychiatrists. When at the age of twelve the time came for a move to the senior department at Besford Court, John would still find himself comfortably housed on a fine estate with a farm, gardens, and craft-rooms. Holidays were often spent at home and there was no suggestion that he openly resented his lot or was un-happy. What did this changed environment do for the boy? His records, which vary little throughout six years of schooling, give a picture cf a healthy, well-grown child, with no physical handicap except a thick mumbling speech, which improved as he grew to adolescence. He was noted as rather timid and docile, and apparently friendly towards the staff, but he showed two persistent characteristics which were to prove much more significant later than they appeared in his childhood. He was always a 'solitary' who made no friends, and he took correction very badly, going off to sulk by himself if scolded. Unfortunately the only really sinister episode at the school was not reported to the Administrator until after the trial. One of the officers owned some prize geese and one morning two of them were found strangled. Young Straffen, who was then about fourteen, was strongly suspected, but for lack of positive proof no action was taken and no entry was made on his records.

When Straffen became sixteen, the school authorities decided to recommend his discharge, though he could have been kept until eighteen under their regulations if he had been certified under the Mental Deficiency Act. He had made poor progress and was at least five years retarded educationally, had shown no aptitude for any craft, and was clearly 'certifiable'. However, it was considered that he might be able to make good as an unskilled or even semi-skilled labourer, as thousands of a similar intellectual level are doing every day, and it was also felt that family life might help his mental development. His I.Q. was then 64 per cent on what is known as the Terman-Merrill 'M' Scale, and his mental age nine years and six months. The headmaster's final report on leaving ran as follows:

Well-behaved and amenable to discipline but physically not too robust. Inclined to be nervous and timid. Takes little part in games and is not gifted in the use of tools. Is still backward and appears incapable of much improvement. Is fond of working at odd jobs not calling for physical strength and prefers his own company usually.

Might be capable of light work not calling for too much effort or intelligence but will need sympathetic handling for a time.

*

So Straffen came back to his family in Bath in March 1946, to have a try at standing on his own feet among normal people. He was examined by the Medical Officer of Health, who agreed that he was still certifiable under the Mental Deficiency Act. It was unfortunate, but understandable in the depleted condition of the Public Health Department at the time, that he was not put under any of the forms of supervision the law allows for known defectives. But after a few false starts in industry it looked for a time as though the lad would do well. He found a congenial job as machinist in a clothing factory and kept it for ten months, leaving of his own accord when he was already deep in trouble, for at some time early in 1947 for reasons wholly unknown Straffen had begun to go off the rails. The form his delinquency took was so unusual and profitless that a psychologist might well suspect some deep unconscious motive. He started to steal small articles (apparently mainly from unoccupied houses) and seems to have hidden them if he could not dispose of them. He neither gave them away nor took them home. His mother states that nothing whatever was known of his exploits. Usually a defective boy starts serious stealing under the influence of lads of higher intelligence, but characteristically Straffen did his jobs entirely alone and had no companion, good or bad.

On 27 July 1947 occurred an incident much canvassed later. A complaint was made to the police that John had assaulted a thirteen-year-old girl (as far as is known, a stranger to him) by putting his hand over her mouth and saying, 'What would you do if I killed you? I have done it before.' At the time this must have seemed like a piece of childish horseplay, but in the light of subsequent events it becomes significant of the dangerous lines on which the boy's thoughts were running. Six weeks later the police were told that Straffen had strangled five chickens belonging to the father of another girl with whom he had had a quarrel, and had left their carcasses in the fowl house. This episode might presumably have led to a charge but for the fact that the police had already come across evidence connecting him with a housebreaking offence, and Straffen obligingly informed them of thirteen others of which he had not been suspected. His history and his childishly confiding and boastful behaviour after arrest led to a remand in custody for psychiatric examination. After the Medical Officer to Horfield Prison had given a certificate that he was a feeble-minded person, he was committed at the Bath Quarter Sessions on 10 October 1947 to Hortham Colony (Bristol) under Section 8 (b) of the Mental Deficiency Act 1913.

The authorities at Hortham Colony have been much criticized for not keeping a dangerous defective in custody once they had hold of him, but they had no evidence at the time that Straffen was a dangerous defective. The certificate on which he was admitted stated specifically that he was 'not of violent or dangerous propensities', and the only charge against him known to the colony authorities was one of housebreaking. The institution is an 'open' colony which specializes in the training and ultimate resettlement in the community of high-grade defectives, who are, of course, not admitted unless they have given some evidence of failure to maintain themselves or to live inoffensively in the outer world. From every point of view Straffen appeared to be a suitable case for what is now called 'rehabilitation'. As at Besford Court, he proved well-behaved and amenable to the mild discipline of the place, except that he absconded on several occasions for short periods. He was considered timid and nervous rather than aggressive, never cruel to animals, and without any interest in girls; he did not even bother to go to colony dances. At simple jobs in the colony or in neighbouring market gardens he proved a steady worker. But once again it was noted that he had no friends.

After about twenty months in the colony, Straffen was licensed in July 1949 to an agricultural hostel for defectives at Winchester, where he did well at first, but blotted his record after a few months by stealing a bag of walnuts. This led to the revocation of his licence and a recall to Hortham in February 1950. In August he was in mild trouble again for going home without leave and violently resisting the police when captured. (In view of his later history it is only fair to the Bath police to say that this seems to have been a mere tussle. Straffen arrived back in the colony next day in excellent form and without bruising.) Probably he learned from his experience that escapes got him nowhere, for he steadied down so well that home leave for a few days was granted in February 1951. Having taken this opportunity to find a job with a market gardener near Bath, he was allowed to keep it and was formally licensed to the care of his mother, though his father was living in the home. The house, which had always been clean and well-kept, was in a good part of Bath and was now less crowded as the family had taken in extra rooms, and John's elder brother was on the premises and anxious to keep him on the right path. The staff of the Public Health Department were at hand with sympathetic supervision.

One acute disappointment fell on Straffen about this time. According to the provisions of the Mental Deficiency Act, he had to be seen by the Visitors to Hortham Colony on attaining the age of twenty-one (a sensible regulation made to prevent the unnecessary detention of mental defectives) and, as he was considered by them as still 'in need of care and control', his certificate was renewed for another five years. This did not mean that he was recalled to Hortham Colony, but that he was still 'on a string'. His mother appealed to the Board of Control, and a further examination by Dr Astley Weston, the Medical Officer of Health for Bath, who knew the case well, was ordered for 10 July. This time things went better. Dr Weston certainly confirmed the diagnosis of mental deficiency, but he estimated the lad's age to be ten years (it had for many years been assessed at nine and a half) and advised that the present trial on licence should be renewed for another six months, 'at the end of which period he might be considered for discharge'. This was the best news Straffen had had yet and it looked as though Hortham had made another success with an 'unstable defective'. He was working steadily and he gave the impression of a well-set-up, almost normal young man. He realized that his future freedom depended, however, on favourable reports on his work and honesty, and this fact he seems to have passionately resented.

*

10 July 1951, the day of the Medical Officer of Health's examination was, after all, an unlucky day for Straffen and the beginning of a long, tragic sequence of events. At Windsor a litle girl named Christine Butcher was found strangled with the belt of her own raincoat and the Press was full for weeks after, not only with details of the crime, but of the unsuccessful efforts of the police to find the murderer. How could this pitiful tragedy affect the life of a feeble-minded youth in Bath, who had never been near Windsor or known the child? It seems that Straffen had for long harboured deeply rooted vicious impulses which his natural timidity kept from outward expression, and his very limited intelligence was unable to correct or restrain by normal reasoning. Chief among these smouldering hatreds was an intense resentment against the police, who had, he was later to explain to psychiatrists and to his family, been responsible for all his troubles since he was a child of eight. Matters had become worse in recent years, for a curious reason relating to his arrest in 1947. He had then talked boastfully and loosely to the prison psychiatrists and to the police about his misdeeds, including alleged sex offences, and the recipients of these confidences had reacted differently, according to their different professional trainings. The psychiatrists

were impressed by Straffen's imperfect moral sense; the police were naturally more interested in him as a potential criminal of an unusually irresponsible and mischievous type. As a result Straffen had, when on licence from Hortham, been subjected occasionally to police inquiries about his movements (such an episode had occurred that summer), which had aroused in him a furious, though well-concealed, desire for revenge. That these unwelcome attentions were the result of his own behaviour his feeble intelligence could not grasp. If police action endangered his freedom, he could only blame the police. It was a most unfortunate coincidence that strangling had already appealed to Straffen as a safe means of vengeance; whether he derived other emotional satisfactions from the act is uncertain, but he may well have done so as it is a well recognized sexual substitute. Here in the Windsor case was an example where death by strangling was obviously giving the maximum amount of trouble to his enemies, the police – and at no cost to the murderer. It was a final and horrible disaster that the affections of this strange being had always been reserved entirely for his own family; the life of an unknown little girl meant nothing to him at all.

A glance at the flaring headlines of the Sunday newspapers for 15 July 1951 will suggest that thoughts of Christine's tragedy may well have been passing through the wretched youth's head as he set out for his usual solitary Sunday afternoon visit to the cinema, though how far he had then formulated a definite murder plan can never be known. It was by a most cruel mischance that his route should take him past the meadow where five-year-old Brenda Goddard had wandered unobserved to gather flowers. She was a carefully guarded little girl, adored by her foster-parents, Mr and Mrs Pullen, who wanted to adopt her legally, and by her widowed mother who worked in Bath and visited her frequently. Her absence from the Pullens' garden, where she had been sent to play, was quickly noted and the search began in a matter of minutes. All that is known of her end is derived from Straffen's own statement. Apparently he offered to show the child a place where she could find better flowers, and so winning was his manner with children that she allowed him to lift her over a fence into a little copse. There his hands closed round her throat, and, for the strange reason that 'she did not scream', he bashed her head against a stone. The murderer continued on his way and spent the rest of the afternoon happily at the pictures, munching sweets and watching a film called *Shockproof*. Truly, his mental detachment from his fellow human beings, and from normal human feelings, went deeper than any teacher or psychiatrist had guessed.

It says much for the shrewdness of the Bath police that directly the child's body was found (it had been left where it lay without any attempt at concealment), Straffen was placed high on the list of suspects. Contrary to later rumours, the lad had no local reputation as a strangler of animals or as a molester of children; even the two minor episodes arising out of quarrels with girls were unknown to the neighbours.

At first there was nothing whatever to connect him with the crime. Indeed, as is only too common in child murders, there was no clue of any sort. Questioned at the station by the officers he knew only too well, Straffen was calm and apparently cooperative and he admitted quite freely that he was the man in blue seen in the street by the foster-mother Mrs Pullen, when she ran out to hunt for Brenda. But that circumstance alone could not justify an arrest, it could only heighten suspicion, and Straffen would have gone free as the Windsor murderer has done if the devils in his feeble brain had not driven him on to further villainies.

It happened that in the course of their inquiries over Brenda's death, the police had visited Straffen's employer at the market garden to check his movements. This gentleman, who had been latterly less satisfied with his work and behaviour, took occasion to discharge him on 31 July. Rightly or wrongly, the lad attributed his dismissal to the action of the police, and his twisted mind registered it as a new grievance calling for a new revenge. And what revenge could be more effective or 'easier', in his own dreadful phrase, than the murder of another little girl? On 8 August he deliberately picked up an older child, Cicely Batstone, aged nine, at a cinema, persuaded her to accompany him to another picture-house, and later to a meadow known as the Tumps, on the outskirts of Bath, where he strangled her. This carefully planned murder had, however, shown up the weakness of the intelligence behind the veneer of cunning. Considering that the police were already hard on his heels for the murder of one child, the notion of murdering a second under their very noses was as demented as it was evil. To make his detection more inevitable, Straffen had taken the child in a bus, where he was certain to be noticed, for every inhabitant of Bath was keyed up to look suspiciously at any man accompanied by a little girl. Later, in the field he selected for his horrible purpose, a courting couple passed so near that they could see him playing with the laughing child. Yet he even stood up to watch them go, before he stooped down to strangle the child – apparently without a thought that he would inevitably be described and identified by them later. (Surely this is coming very near to meeting the classic test of a murderer's responsibility: 'Would he have done it with a policeman at his elbow?') How long he stayed in the field is not known, but after buying some fish and chips for his supper he was home about a quarter past ten.

It was, however, through a source other than the couple in the meadow that the murder was revealed; the story suggests a radio serial rather than sober crime reporting. The wife of a Bath policeman, Constable Cowley, had been walking past the Tumps that evening and had noticed with uneasy suspicion a tall fair young man and a child in a grey cardigan and coloured frock strolling across the field, which she knew to be little frequented. Later the same night she mentioned the episode to her husband, but even if any action had been indicated on such a slight basis, it was too late to do anything until morning. Before seven the next morning came an emergency call for the constable to join in a search for a child reported missing the evening before. When he arrived at the police station and reported his wife's story, one can imagine the horror with which his seniors realized that the child Mrs Cowley had seen was dressed like the missing girl – and the man answered the description of Straffen, a suspect for the previous murder! Not a moment was lost, though they could have had little hope in their hearts. A police car called for Mrs Cowley and, under her guidance, sped to the place where she had seen those ominous companions. Directly the body was found, officers were dispatched to pick up Straffen, who had not yet risen from a sound night's rest.

When questioned at the station Straffen made confused and childish statements. He had left the little girl asleep in the field . . . he had left her dead but he hadn't killed her – and so forth. A little later he proceeded light-heartedly to a confession of the Brenda Goddard murder and even demonstrated on a sergeant how it was done. As far as could be ascertained then or later, neither murder had aroused more feeling in him than killing a rabbit. When he was charged the police felt obliged to warn him of the serious position he was in, at which he laughed and retorted, 'She is dead, but you cannot prove I did it.' He pointed out that a courting couple had been in the field, too. There is some reason to think, from his subsequent answers to queries, that, although Straffen had grasped the meaning of the word 'witness' up to a point, he confused it with 'eye-witness' and thought he could suffer no penalty for either murder as no one had actually seen him commit the crime.

Straffen was charged with the murder of Cicely Batstone at the Taunton Assizes on 17 October 1951 before Mr Justice Oliver. In view of his long history as a certified defective, of the purposeless nature of the murder, and of his completely irresponsible attitude when on a capital charge, it was decided by the prosecution to raise the question of his mental condition on arraignment rather than later. As the law stands, it does not necessarily follow that because a prisoner has shown signs of mental abnormality he will be considered 'unfit to plead'. The point is decided by a jury sworn by a special oath, and as insanity is and always has been an ill-defined term, certain traditional rules have been laid down to guide the members. In the first place it should be clear that the issue is the mental condition of the prisoner at the time of trial, not at the time of the offence. He must be considered unable to understand the nature of the proceedings in Court, to follow the evidence intelligently, to distinguish between a plea of guilty and not guilty, to be incapable of instructing Counsel on his behalf. If the plea of 'unfitness' is accepted the prisoner is held to be insane on arraignment and is sentenced to be detained during Her Majesty's Pleasure. The question of his guilt or innocence never having been tried out, if his mental condition improves he may, in theory, be brought up for trial, but in practice this does not happen.

In Straffen's case the Court seems to have had no difficulty in finding him 'insane on arraignment'. Having been committed to Broadmoor he would normally have disappeared for ever from the public scene. It is the function of Broadmoor to draw the curtain on the last act of tragedies, but in this case there was a terrible and un-precedented epilogue.

*

It is an old and admirable tradition of the Home Office, continued by the Ministry of Health, that the privacy of any persons under detention at Broadmoor shall be rigidly respected. Even if criminal, they are nevertheless among the afflicted of God; it would be an indecency to expose their mental deformities to public gaze or to allow their restricted lives to become an occasion for idle and probably malicious gossip. (That so little use has been made of the unique material these extraordinary Broadmoor patients might provide for serious scientific study of mental disorder is another matter.) So we know very little of Straffen's life within the sheltering walls, except for the few details which emerged at the trial. He would certainly have a full medical and psychological examination on admission, for that is the routine for all inmates. At one of the early interviews with the medical staff an opportunity, which he was under no obligation to accept, would be given to discuss the crimes which had brought him where he was: thereafter, the matter would only be raised on his own initiative. We know that Straffen learned the rules of Contract Bridge and that he was well-behaved. From statements he made later, it would seem that he discussed very fully with other patients the minor technicalities of trials, and the possibility of escape. Somehow or other he picked up the idea that, even if recaptured, he could never be sent back to Broadmoor. Characteristically, he managed to conceal his intense hatred of the place and resentment against those responsible for his confinement.

Straffen had never been a craftsman – though he had had plenty of opportunity of becoming one at the institutions at which he had been trained. He was a horticultural or agricultural labourer and Broadmoor would give him ample scope in his own field but, like all able-bodied inmates of a mental hospital, he would have to take his share of indoor cleaning. So it came about that one beautiful April afternoon, about six months after admission, he was sent under the charge of one of the older attendants to assist another patient in cleaning certain outbuildings known as 'the surgery'. These rooms opened at the back on to a small yard bounded by a ten-foot outer wall of the hospital; against this outer wall stood a low shed some eight and a half feet high with a sloping roof. Some large empty disinfectant tins were lying about in the yard. This tempting layout had attracted the attention of Straffen – or of some other patient who had brought it to his notice – and here, in his own words, is what happened:

'Yesterday afternoon (29 April) I went to the surgery to work. I did one room and then I got a duster and went to Mr Cash and asked him if I could go out and shake the duster. I was out about two minutes and then another patient came out and asked me if I had finished shaking the duster. I said, "I have just finished off now", and he went back in. I then climbed the roof and then I jumped over the wall and ran. . . .'

The time was 2.25 p.m. The fugitive had had the foresight to gain illicit access to his civilian clothes and wear them under his working jeans, so he was not hampered by a distinctive dress. He seems to have had no money. It was not certain what lead he had, but it was sufficient to enable him to get clear away. He would have learnt from his fellow-inmates that, in their anxiety not to alarm the neighbourhood, the authorities at Broadmoor had provided no system whatever for warning of an escape – no sirens, no road blocks, no telephone messages to post-offices or schools. Some twenty minutes after he had got over the wall, Straffen was confident enough to approach a house and beg the occupier, Mrs Spencer, for a drink of water. The ample woods of pine and rhododendrons and the meadow paths of this lovely countryside gave him plenty of cover against pursuit, and by 4.30 he had reached Farley Hill, a small village of some 300 inhabitants about seven miles from Broadmoor. At this hour he was noticed by a Mrs Sims, wife of a local estate worker, into whose life he was to bring unimagined sorrow, and by Mr Barker who lived in the tiny High Street. He must have hung about the outskirts of the village for fully an hour, for at about 5 p.m. he overheard a conversation between Mr Sims and his five-year-old step-daughter, Linda Bowyer, outside the village store. At 5.30 Mr Barker looked out of his window in the High Street and again saw Straffen, now loitering near the village school while Linda was riding up and down the road on her bicycle. A Miss Saxby also saw her a few minutes later. There follows a gap of about twenty minutes, both in Straffen's own narrative and in the evidence of witnesses. One of the Crown witnesses (Mrs Chadwick) who passed that way a little after 5.30 testified that Linda was nowhere about, and she was never seen alive again.

At 5.45 or 5.50 p.m. Straffen reappeared at Farley Hill House, a detached residence about a quarter of a mile across the fields from the village; he was thirsty and begged a glass of water from Miss Jahn, a German children's nurse. According to his own statement he reached the house by walking round by the road, but this would have taken him longer than the twenty minutes interval fixed by the evidence of Mr Barker and Miss Jahn; moreover, Miss Jahn had first caught sight of him coming out of the wood at the side of the house and not along the road. Why had Straffen lied about his route while keeping to the exact truth about the rest of his wanderings? Obviously because the field path between the village High Street and Farley Hill House led past the spots where Linda's bicycle and her strangled

199

body were shortly to be found. This simple technique of accounting meticulously for his movements except for the brief period when he was in contact with his victim had served the murderer well in the Brenda Goddard case.

In a talk over a cup of tea provided by Mrs Kenyon, the mistress of Farley Hill House, Straffen showed a significant anxiety about the contents of the six o'clock news bulletin. He got directions for reaching the bus stop at Wokingham, and on the road asked two other people to show him the way; then he thumbed a lift from a lady (Mrs Miles) who was driving a car. In her car he made a request to be taken 'to town', but she could only promise to drop him at the Bramshill Hunt bus stop, about two miles from Farley Hill House. Here the chase was to end – too late, alas, to save Linda. As the car approached the stop, Straffen saw men in uniform standing about; he asked if they were police and made a hasty exit from the car. Mrs Miles naturally reported her passenger's suspicious behaviour to one of these men, who were in fact Broadmoor nurses. The staff found him a few minutes later, already ominously surrounded by half a dozen children and, after a brief chase and a violent struggle, he was captured. On the way back to Broadmoor, Straffen remarked that he had escaped in order to prove his innocence. 'I have finished with crime,' he said, which may read as an infantile attempt to forestall suspicions certain to arise when the inevitable discovery was made. He had been a free man for four hours and five minutes.

About half past eleven that evening, Mr and Mrs Sims reported to the Berkshire Constabulary that their little girl, Linda, had vanished. As the police knew that Straffen had been at large in the vicinity, their anxiety can be imagined, and despite darkness a search was started and continued until 2.45 a.m. Dawn found them and their trained dogs at work again under the direction of Detective-Superintendent Crombie. At 5.25 a.m. they discovered, in an open field near the Simses' cottage, the cycle the child had been riding when last seen; a few minutes later her body was found under an oak tree in an adjoining copse. She had died from manual strangulation, there was no sign of sexual interference and no attempt had been made to conceal the corpse. All significant indications that the Bath murderer had been at work again.

Now, Broadmoor is no ordinary territory, and even a police officer can only enter by permission of the Medical Superintendent or on order of the Home Secretary. No difficulty was made, however, when Inspector Francis and Sergeant Lawson arrived at 8 that morning. No one in the institution knew that murder had been committed or even that a child was missing. They found Straffen, who had been badly knocked about during his recapture, still in bed: in carefully chosen, non-committal language, he was asked what he did when he was free and whether he had got into any mischief. His reply was memorable: 'I did not kill her.' When the Inspector told him that there had been no suggestion of anyone being killed, he retorted, 'I know what you policemen are, I know I killed two little children but I did not kill the little girl.' When told that a little girl had, in fact, been killed near where he was recaptured, he said, 'I did not kill the little girl on the bicycle.'

As nothing had been said about a bicycle, a more damning statement could not be imagined and Inspector Francis prudently withdrew from the room to consider the course to be taken. Any policeman to whom a criminal makes a confession or incriminating statement nowadays must feel his head loose on his shoulders, and the situation here was particularly delicate. He had not only to be mindful of the Judges' Rules which would compel him to caution Straffen before further questioning, if he intended to charge him, but he may well have been puzzled by technical complications connected with the status of Broadmoor. It is the law that a warrant of arrest cannot be executed within the confines of a prison, and Broadmoor is a quasi-prison. However, criminal process can be and frequently is executed on a person detained in prison, subject to obtaining a production order from the Home Secretary if the prisoner is required to be removed from the custody of the Governor. Inspector Francis had not of course come armed with any such authority, so what he did was to caution Straffen in the familiar terms and then take at his dictation the following long, remarkably detailed and accurate statement:

Yesterday afternoon I went to the surgery to work. I did one room and then I got a duster and went to Mr Cash and asked him if I could go out and shake the duster. I was out about two minutes and then another patient came out and asked me if I had finished shaking the duster. I said, 'I have just finished off now,' and he went back in. I then climbed the roof and then I jumped over the wall and ran downwards towards the road. I climbed over a fence into some woods. I went through the woods and saw a road and I ran down. I got down the bottom of the road. I crossed the road and went down a lane. I got to the end of the lane. I saw a woman outside her house. I asked her for a cup of water. She gave me a cup of water and a cup of tea. When I had drunk that I asked her which way I could get through the woods to the village. She told me. I went through the woods and came out near a school. I think it is Crowthorne. I walked down the street and crossed the road and turned down another road. There was a shoe shop near the corner. I went down this road and saw two men on bikes. They turned round and came back and I dived through the woods. I came from the woods on to a golf course. I climbed up towards the railway lines. I saw two staff at the far end and then I climbed over the wire and run through some people's gardens. I then crossed the road into some more woods. I then walked right through the woods. Then I walked up a path in the woods. I saw some people by a house near the main road. I crossed the main road into some more woods. I saw a man near a house; I think he was blind. I asked him which way

I could get through the woods. He told me to go on one way but I went the opposite way. After about two or three minutes I came to another path. I then came to a private house. I walked through the grounds. I climbed into a field. I kept to the fields for a long time after that. I then came to a main road near a village. I went into another field and kept in the field for about two minutes. I then walked up the hill. I saw a pub on top of the hill. I saw about four little girls talking in the road not far from the pub. One of the little girls ran into her house crying, and the other two went towards the pub. The other one went back to her house and when I looked back she had a bike and was riding up behind me. I heard a man, I think he was from the shop, ask her if her mother was at home. I think she said 'Yes'. The man then got into a van which was parked outside the shop. I then walked straight along the road. I turned round again. The girl was not there at all. I then went to a house along the road past the shop. I went to the house. I saw a woman and two children outside on the lawn. I put my hand up and she came over to me. I asked her for a drink of water. She gave me a drop of water. Another woman in the house asked me if I would like a cup of tea. I said 'Yes'. She gave me a pot of tea, milk, sugar, and biscuits and brought me out the newspaper. She then left me to read my newspaper and have my tea. When I had finished I took all the stuff back inside the house and asked how far was the nearest town. I asked her if she had a wireless. She told me she had one but the battery had gone. I then closed the door and left. I then went on towards the road away from the shop and turned right. I got about ten to fifteen yards. I saw a man in a field and asked him where was the nearest town. He told me about six miles. I asked him what time the buses were running, and he told me, 'There's one about ten past seven that night.' I told him I had got plenty of time. I then walked down the road which he told me. I met two more people and asked them which was the quickest way to the bus stop. They told me to take the left road; there were two roads where I was speaking to them. I went down the left-hand road, then I saw a man on a bike. I said 'Good afternoon' to him, and he said the same to me. I walked down towards the main road. A lorry came along. I tried to get a lift.

He did not stop. After about five minutes another car came down. I put up my hand and she stopped. She asked me which way I was going. I said, 'Towards the town.' She gave me a lift and I was speaking to her in the car. She asked me if I was a foreigner. I said 'No'. I told her I came from Hampshire and told her I lived in Winchester. I did not speak no more. After that she dropped me by a pub and I got out. She told me a bus would come along. I saw her stop again, and I saw her speak to the staff, so I ran through the pub. I came out on a field. I saw some children in the field so I climbed through in to the Army Barracks. I came back into the same field again. I saw the children again. I looked towards the main road. The children got frightened, they wondered what it was about, so I climbed into another field then and ran. I saw the staff coming from the other fields. I climbed through another wire fence then which led into some woods. After about two minutes I climbed up a bank and hid. The staff then came and caught me. I have been shown a photograph by the police officer of a little girl and that is a photo of the little girl who I saw with the bike near the pub and who followed me up the road.

After it had been read over to Straffen and signed by him, a curious incident happened. He was asked if he objected to scrapings being taken from under his nails. He said 'No', but added, 'You are cunning, aren't you? You are looking for flesh – they did that to me before – but you will be unlucky this time !' On examination, his nails showed signs of recent and ruthless biting – so much so that no scrapings could be taken from the right hand. Thus, on his own admission, Straffen had anticipated this test and prepared for it before he could have known (if he had been innocent) that a murder had been committed.

Next day, 1 May, Straffen was arrested and charged with the murder of Linda Bowyer, his statement having been checked up by Detective-Superintendent Crombie with remarkable rapidity and thoroughness. By now the necessary authorization had been obtained from the Home Secretary, who had been consulted throughout and had given his consent to the steps taken in this unique situation. If not the first, this was nearly the first instance of a judicial process being executed on a person detained in Broadmoor.

On the morning of 2 May 1952 Straffen appeared before the Reading County Magistrates sitting at the Assize Court, Reading. When his name was called he stumbled up the steps of the dock handcuffed to a police officer and looking considerably the worse for his struggle for liberty. Chief Inspector Francis gave evidence that after the warrant for arrest had been read over to Straffen he said: 'I did not kill her; that's a frame-up, that is.' When charged that morning Straffen said: 'I don't care, it is a frame-up.' Inspector Brazell, appearing for the Director of Public Prosecutions, informed the Magistrates that he had been instructed to ask for legal aid for the prisoner, whereupon the following dialogue took place:

The Clerk: Do you wish to be legally represented?
Straffen: Yes.
The Clerk: Do you want a legal aid certificate?
Straffen: Yes.
The Clerk: Do you understand what I am asking?
Straffen: Yes.
The Clerk: Have you any particular solicitor you would like instructed, or will you leave it to the Magistrates?
Straffen (after a short pause): The Magistrates.
The Chairman (The Hon. David Smith): A legal aid certificate will be granted and counsel made available.

After a further remand Straffen, now represented by a solicitor, Mr Brown, was ultimately committed on 9 May to take his trial at the Summer Assizes at Winchester.

Another of the numerous minor legal problems connected with this unique case cropped up over his custody while on remand. The Order under which he was detained in Broad-moor had been made by Mr Justice Oliver at the Taunton Assizes in October 1951, when he had been found unfit to plead on an indictment for murder, and as this Order was presumably still valid, it might be assumed that Broadmoor was the only place to which the prisoner could be remanded. After careful consideration, the Magistrates, who had no precedent on which to rely, and were naturally concerned not to act irregularly or in excess of their duty, none the less decided that as the Broadmoor authorities had failed in their duty to hold Straffen safely, it was in the public interest that he should be remanded to a place where further escape was virtually impossible. He was therefore detained in Brixton Prison, and later in Wandsworth: a lad of twenty-one about to be tried for his life for the second time, and for a third murder.

It was inevitable that Straffen's escape should be followed by an outburst of rage and terror on the part of the general public, especially that section of it which lives in the vicinity of Broadmoor. A deeply rooted suspicion that too many sane people find their way into that institution and that the inmates, sane or insane, are too indulgently treated, sprang into vigorous life. How had it come about that a man found 'unfit to plead' in October proved capable of organizing a cunning escape in the following April? Why had a dangerous criminal not been better guarded?

The Berkshire County Council had some eighteen months earlier made representations that the increasing freedom accorded to Broadmoor patients created a dangerous situation for the inhabitants of that County. Now, within a few hours of the tragedy, protests from public bodies, local villagers, and from individuals were pouring into White-hall, the points which aroused particular indignation being the absence of any system for warning the public of escapes, and the wearing of civilian clothes by dangerous patients.

If it had been known that Straffen was at large, not a child in the neighbourhood would have been allowed out of doors and Linda Bowyer would have been alive today. His calls at houses and queries addressed to passers-by would have ensured prompt recapture. To meet these vociferous criticisms, the Minister of Health promptly appointed a Committee to inquire into 'the adequacy of security arrangements at Broadmoor and to make recommendations'. Its report, read in conjunction with the evidence at the trial, unfortunately confirmed the impression that precautions against escape were defective. Obsolete locks; at least one obvious escape route leading over an outer wall; civilian clothes left accessible to dangerous patients; security rules for staff not revised for over forty years and out of print at that – the items add up to a formidable indictment.

The Committee's terms of reference were confined to examination of security arrangements at Broadmoor, but these cannot be fairly discussed without recalling the other complicated problems which confront the authorities there. Founded in 1863 for 'criminal lunatics' whose detention in ordinary jails had long been recognized as a source of abominable hardships, Broadmoor has always housed two classes of inmate. Firstly, those who have been found 'guilty but insane' after trial, or insane on arraignment (i.e. 'unfit to plead') *or* after inquiry by the Home Secretary under the Criminal Lunatics Act 1884 ('pleasure men'); and secondly, a small number who become insane while serving a prison sentence and are transferred to Broadmoor until their sentence expires ('time men'). With the exception of a few who have been, in the classic phrase, 'fortunate in their juries', these people are all mentally sick; whatever their degree of moral guilt, they are primarily in need of medical treatment and are properly regarded by the staff as patients as well as prisoners. If the conditions of life for those behind the walls of Broadmoor have improved out of all knowledge under the care of the recent Medical Superintendent, it is not because they are a specially pampered class, but because modern methods of treatment, both physical and psychological, have revolutionized the position of mental patients. It is unthinkable that in a Christian civilization fellow-creatures should be excluded from the benefits conferred by medical progress on the ground that they have committed crimes – for which they have been held to be not legally responsible!

But this, of course, is not the whole story. As the Committee's Report freely admits, the first, though not the only concern of the Administration in Broadmoor should be the public safety. All amenities devised for the mass of patients, or privileges accorded to individuals, should be considered in this light. It follows that the more the general régime is humanized and rules relaxed, the more necessary it is to separate the sheep from the goats. One gathers from the Report that this necessity is well understood, and that dangerous patients are segregated in well-guarded blocks. Indeed, it is a fact that since 1900 only some twelve men have escaped from Broadmoor, a record which compares favourably with that of other prisons and mental institutions. Unfortunately, the lamentable tale of Straffen's escape leaves too many questions unanswered. If he was classified as a 'dangerous case', then the custody was inefficient; if he was not considered a dangerous case, he ought to have been. A double murderer is surely a potential menace to be guarded with every conceivable care, however well-behaved inside the institution.

It is reassuring to know that there has now been a complete reorganization of the Broadmoor régime and it may be hoped that there will be no repetition of this unhappy episode.

*

On the morning of Monday, 21 July 1952, the trial opened at the Castle, Winchester, before Mr Justice Cassels and a jury. The Solicitor-General, Sir Reginald Manningham-Buller, Q.C., Mr G. D. Roberts, Q.C., and Mr J. Hutchinson appeared for the Crown; Straffen had been granted a Defence Certificate and was represented by Mr Henry Elam and Mr H. E. Park. It is a difficult trial to summarize clearly because of the unusual points of law and procedure which emerged to interrupt its course; the evidence itself was clear and simple.

The first surprise came when, in answer to the charge of murdering Linda Bowyer, the prisoner pleaded 'not guilty'. It should be noted that this was the first time in history that an inmate of Broadmoor had been charged with an offence committed outside the institution; further, this same man had been found 'insane on arraignment' only eight months earlier in respect of a similar charge. The natural supposition had been that he would again be found 'unfit to plead'. Now it was clear that the prisoner was to be tried as a 'sane' man, and that the defence had left the issue of insanity to be raised later in the trial.

After the Solicitor-General had spent seventy minutes in outlining the case for the prosecution and some nine witnesses had been examined, he rose again to ask leave to call evidence on the Bath murders. It is a jealously guarded principle of English Law that the prisoner must have a fair trial on matters covered by the indictment and that 'evidence of similar facts involving the accused might not be dragged in to his prejudice without reasonable cause'. But alleged multiple murders have before now been held to be a 'reasonable cause'. In Straffen's case it could be argued that his admissions to the Bath police showed that he was guilty of the deaths of the two children in Bath, and the circumstances surrounding the murder of Linda Bowyer were so similar that the evidence of the two Bath deaths should be admissible to prove the identity of the murderer of the third child. For the defence, Mr Henry Elam urged that, if such evidence were admitted, it could only result in the creation of prejudice against the accused and might tip the scales against him, adding with much reason, 'never has there been such a case as this one'. After an intricate legal argument had been heard in the absence of the jury, the judge ruled that the evidence was admissible. This was theoretically an extremely important decision and greatly lightened the task of the prosecution (as Straffen and the murdered child had never been actually seen in each other's company), but in fact everyone in the jury-box, and indeed in the kingdom, must have known Straffen's record perfectly well and could not have dismissed it from their minds. The episode had the curious result, as the Press had not been excluded from Court and were of course allowed to print the gist of the legal argument, that the jury learned from their morning papers the nature of the evidence they were to hear later on in the day.

But not the same jury! For on the second morning of the trial the great sensation broke. Judge and counsel were nearly an hour late coming into Court and, when they did, the judge addressed the surprised jurors as follows:

'You will remember that last night I warned you very earnestly that you should not discuss this case with anyone. Owing to the alleged conduct of one of your members, which has been reported to the Court, I am compelled very reluctantly, and with very great regret, to discharge you from any further dealings with this case. I must request you to remain in Court until that matter has been properly investigated. After it has been investigated and the Court has indicated the course it proposes to take maybe some of you will be required in another Court for service with another jury. Therefore, I am afraid you must cease to act as a jury in this case.'

Here was a tiresome set-back to the solemn course of justice! A second jury was sworn in and the Solicitor-General was put to the necessity of repeating his lengthy opening address while numerous members of the Berkshire Constabulary had to be taken off their proper duties to trace the witnesses who had already given evidence and bring them back to repeat their stories in Court. After the lunch interval the first jury was lined up and a resident of Southsea, who had been brought hot-foot from Portsmouth by the police, pointed out one of the jurors as the man who had informed an enthralled audience in a political club in Southsea the previous evening that he was on the jury in the Straffen case, that in his opinion the accused was not guilty, and, further, that in his opinion one of the witnesses called for the prosecution had committed the murder. This indiscreet individual, who seems to have left little unsaid that he ought not to have said, was ordered by the judge to remain in the precincts of the Court until the end of the case. The penalty gave him sufficient leisure, one hopes, to meditate on the terms of a juryman's oath – ('to try the issues between our Sovereign Lady the Queen and the Prisoner at the Bar and a true verdict give *according to the evidence*') – and also on the four hundred pounds his careless talk had cost the county. Moreover, as the judge reminded him when at the end of the trial his counsel appeared to offer a full apology on his behalf, this 'wrong and wicked' indiscretion had entailed the recalling of the mother of the murdered child 'to tell again her sorry and pathetic story'.

The evidence of the earlier witnesses for the prosecution did little more than fill in the details of Straffen's own narrative of the escape and subsequent wanderings, with which the reader is already familiar. The Court at Winchester must have got a vivid picture of the peaceful English countryside on an unseasonably hot day in spring – kindly ladies give a thirsty wayfarer cups of still-rationed tea; an old man gathers savoury herbs in a ditch; the passage of time is measured only by television or the news bulletins; the village children play in the quiet lanes until dusk while their parents await their return without anxiety . . . An incongruous setting for this ugly tragedy. As for the Bath witnesses to the first two murders, much of their evidence was new as the cases had not been tried out at the Taunton Assizes, and it profoundly moved the Court.

Only if one compares British trials with those of other countries does one realize what a beautiful piece of craftsmanship is a 'case for the prosecution', such as the spectators saw it at Winchester. Presumably the credit is to be divided between the Director of Public Prosecutions' Department and the Berkshire police. The one remaining loose end in the network surrounding Straffen was tied up by a police sergeant who had, with his little boy, walked the path that the murderer must have taken from Farley High Street to the copse and on to Farley Hill House. They had done the journey in six and a half minutes. So Straffen's unaccounted-for twenty minutes would have given him ample time to accost the child, take her into the privacy of the wood and kill her, and make his way on to Farley Hill House; ample time indeed for a man who knew the horrible routine so well. (In April the copse had been a glorious mass of blue-bells. Had he used the same bait of flower-picking that had brought Brenda Goddard to her death?)

Some more of those minor points of law peculiar to this case came up when evidence was being given of the police interview with Straffen in Broadmoor. Mr Elam challenged the admissibility of the replies given to Inspector Francis's initial queries on how he had spent his time during his freedom, on the ground that persons *in custody* should not, by the Judges' Rules, be questioned without the usual caution having been administered – and Straffen being a

Broadmoor patient was technically 'in custody'. Fortunately, Mr Justice Cassels took the common-sense view, subsequently approved by the Court of Criminal Appeal, that 'custody' means in custody of the police. Another hope for the defence faded.

When Mr Henry Elam rose to open the defence, there could have been little doubt in the mind of anyone in Court that Straffen's guilt had been firmly established. Only two of his witnesses, in fact, had evidence of any importance. A Mrs Tanner and her brother Mr Crouch had heard what they thought might be the scream of a child outside their home and coming from the copse where Linda's body was later found, at 6.45 on the evening of the murder. As Straffen was at this time again in custody, the incident might have raised serious doubts as to his guilt, but it emerged in cross-examination that the sound had at first been taken for the squeal of a pig and the direction from which it appeared to come was very uncertain. Obviously Straffen's only hope of avoiding a death sentence lay in establishing that his mental condition would justify a verdict of 'guilty but insane'.

In order to understand how formidable was Mr Elam's task it is necessary to give a brief account of the legal position of a mental defective charged with murder. No statutory provision has been made for him. Ever since 1913, Section 8 of the Mental Deficiency Act has empowered a Court to refrain from sentencing a mental defective on conviction and to send him to an institution instead, but this law only applies to prisoners liable to be sentenced to a term of *imprisonment*; it is not applicable to capital cases. So counsel's one hope was to bring his client within the four corners of the McNaghten Rules, which were not designed to cover mental deficiency and take no cognizance of varying degrees of responsibility.

The relevant passage from the Rules must be familiar to every reader: it runs as follows:

To establish a defence on the grounds of insanity it must be clearly proved that, at the time of committing the act, the party accused was labouring under such a defect of reason from disease of the mind, as not to know the nature and quality of the act he was doing, or, if he did know it, that he did not know what he was doing was wrong.

By some authorities it is even held to be doubtful whether the famous Rules are applicable to defectives, as amentia (mental deficiency) is not technically a 'disease of the mind', but the Report of the Royal Commission on Capital Punishment points out that this has never been a practical obstacle:

When a defence of insanity put forward by a mental defective is rejected, usually this is not because the Court rules that mental deficiency is not a disease of the mind, but because the jury are not satisfied that the accused did not know the nature and quality of the act, or did not know it was wrong;

in other words, that the case does not come within the legal limits of criminal responsibility.

As common sense would suggest, if a defective with a low I.Q., an idiot or an imbecile, commits a murder there is no hesitation in regarding him as unfit to plead, and both Broadmoor and Rampton Institution have contained several unhappy inmates of this type. But a much greater difficulty arises if the prisoner is feeble-minded, i.e. with a mental age of seven or over; 'it will seldom be possible to maintain that he did not know that what he was doing was forbidden by law'. Certainly it would be impossible to maintain these two propositions concerning John Straffen: the evidence showed that he had deliberately set out to kill little girls, and he had himself repeatedly stated that he did it 'to spite the police', i.e. *because* he knew it was against the law. Moreover, the histories of the murders of Cicely Batstone and Linda

Bowyer as unfolded in Court showed considerable cunning and deliberation; he had picked up many legal terms from fellow-patients and seemed to understand them, he had tried to forestall adverse evidence which might have been obtained from scrapings under his finger nails. His statements revealed a photographic memory; Detective-Superintendent Crombie, a highly experienced officer, had followed his tracks with meticulous care and had been able to confirm them in every detail. The judge at the Taunton Assizes had pointed out to the jury that 'one might as well try a baby in arms' as a defective. Straffen's mentality was obviously far removed from that of a baby, and the fact that he was really comparable to a nine-or-ten-year-old schoolboy would help him very little.

Before we turn to the evidence of the six psychiatrists and prison medical officers who were called to enlighten the jury, it would be well to refer to three special handicaps (two of which are still present) experienced by any doctor who gives evidence in Court on a mental defective. The first is the unfamiliarity of counsel and jury with what mental deficiency means in practice. Many of them may never have seen, and fewer still have conversed with, a feeble-minded person identified as such, and they are easily misled by a practically normal appearance and a glib use of a small vocabulary. The second is the difficulty of quoting any decisive test which would place the high-grade defective once and for all outside the category of normal people. The third is the confusion between insanity and mental deficiency which the law of murder at that date made inevitable. A conscientious doctor had to say that the patient was *not* insane, however defective he might be, because in fact the two conditions are wholly different, a fact which the law recognized by prescribing two totally different methods of certification in separate Acts. But in the murder trial of a defective person he had to support a plea for a verdict of 'guilty but insane' and finally to listen to the judge telling the jury that they must consider whether the prisoner was '*insane* within the meaning of the criminal law, *not* that he was feeble-minded'! No wonder that members of an excusably bewildered jury sometimes failed to understand what a doctor was trying to tell them and became suspicious of his *bona fides*. The position was as though a doctor could not get his child suffering from measles into hospital unless he called the disease scarlet fever. Anyone reading the trial of Straffen would find it hard to imagine that mental deficiency was a well-established entity, that intelligence tests are of proved diagnostic value, and that the diminished responsibility of defectives, for every other crime but murder, had been recognized by the law for forty years.

Today, Section 2 of the Homicide Act 1957 has greatly simplified the situation, for it makes definite provision for accused murderers of 'diminished responsibility'. The Section is so drafted that it clearly covers the class of 'mental defectives' to which Straffen belongs:

2. (1) Where a person kills or is a party to the killing of another, he shall not be convicted of murder if he was suffering from such abnormality of mind (whether arising from a condition of arrested or retarded development of mind or any inherent causes or induced by disease or injury) as substantially impaired his mental responsibility for his acts and omissions in doing or being a party to the killing.

(2) On a charge of murder it shall be for the defence to prove that the person charged is by virtue of this section not liable to be convicted of murder.

(3) A person who but for this section would be liable, whether as principal or as an accessary, to be convicted of murder shall be liable instead to be convicted of manslaughter.

The doctrine of 'diminished responsibility' has been evolved over some eighty years in Scotland and had been generally acknowledged to work very well. Its application in the English Courts is causing some anxiety but it is certainly an improvement on the clumsy procedure for the defence of a high-grade mentally defective murderer with which Straffen's counsel had to contend.

The three doctors who appeared for the defence were not only experienced psychiatrists and prison medical officers, but had seen much more of the prisoner than is usual with expert witnesses, two of them in connexion with his Bath record, and one through daily contact with him in Broadmoor. It was not the least remarkable feature of this remarkable case that they were not only in complete agreement with each other, but showed no real divergence from the opinions expressed by the three medical specialists called in rebuttal by the Crown. All of them found that Straffen was a 'feeble-minded' person, still certifiable as such under the Mental Deficiency Acts and 'that his powers of control and his judgement were not up to those of a normal person'. But all had also to agree that the prisoner knew he was killing the children, and he knew it was wrong; only the emphasis varied in the different medical testimonies.

It was significant of the difficulties surrounding this question of criminal responsibility that the reaction of the listeners in Court to the expert witnesses varied greatly. Their insistence that Straffen's understanding of what he was doing should be measured by the limits of his intelligence was irritating and absurd to some; to others it was a fair and accurate statement of the patient's mental condition. The latest examiner to test Straffen, Dr Murdoch, Principal Medical officer of Wandsworth Prison, had found him the most closely approximating to normal in his answers. This may be due to a late improvement in intelligence, of which Straffen had previously shown some signs, or simply to the fact that even a defective learns in time to know what answers are expected of him. The number of psychological tests and psychiatric examinations Straffen has had in his short life must be approaching three figures.

With the evidence of Dr Murdoch the procession of witnesses ended and Mr Elam and the Solicitor-General made their closing speeches. The defence rested mainly on the absence of a direct link between Straffen and the child: the Solicitor-General's attack concentrated on the Bath murders and the fact that Straffen's mental condition did not justify his being brought within the scope of the McNaghten Rules. The same points were made by Mr Justice Cassels in his very lucid and detailed summing-up, which occupied some three hours and forty minutes. In dealing with the mental issue, he said: 'It does not follow that if any patient escapes from Broadmoor he may commit murder with impunity. Whether he has escaped from Broadmoor or whether he has never been near such an institution the law is the same; the question which the jury has to ask itself, and to answer, is the same: was he at the time he committed his act insane within the meaning of the Criminal Law?'

In view of the evidence there could be only one answer. The jury, consisting of ten men and two women, took only twenty-nine minutes to arrive at their verdict. There was a delay of another twenty-five minutes while the judge was fetched from his lodgings, before they filed back into the jury-box. It is said that jurors who have brought in a verdict of guilty on a capital charge never look at the prisoner on their return to Court, and now it was observed that not one of them glanced towards the dock where Straffen, in his shapeless prison suit, towered head and shoulders over four warders. He looked, not at the jury who were to decide his fate, but at the judge: with mouth agape he heard the fatal 'Guilty'. The expression on his face did not change as he watched the square of black cloth being placed on the judge's head and listened to the traditional sentence. Still without apparent emotion, he was touched on the shoulder by a warder and shuffled out of the dock.

*

The date of execution was fixed for 6 September 1952, but on 29 August, Sir David Maxwell Fyfe, the Home Secretary, announced that he had recommended to Her Majesty that a reprieve be granted and that Straffen would not be returned to Broadmoor. Thus for a second time in twelve months, John Thomas Straffen was made the subject of an Order by the Crown; first that he should be detained in Broadmoor, and then that he should not be hanged.

By order of the Secretary of State a formal inquiry under the Criminal Lunatics Act 1884 had been held, and the prisoner had been examined by three psychiatric specialists, who had not previously seen him. Their advice would certainly have influenced the Home Secretary's decision. It was not a popular reprieve. The horror of the crimes, especially of the third murder, had profoundly impressed the public and it was widely felt that the murderer had given sufficient evidence of responsibility to justify the authorities in leaving him for execution. The ordinary citizen does not like to think that criminals condemned in open Court by a judge and jury should be let out, so to speak, by a side-door into Harley Street. Those who place great emphasis on the deterrent effect of capital punishment, and hold that only the death penalty is commensurate with the gravity of the offence of taking human life, would not hesitate to hang even a certified defective.

The advocates of mercy had, however, a strong case. Although there are, as the Report on Capital Punishment points out (p. 121), wide variations of mental capacity and of responsibility among mental defectives, it would be contrary to the bulk of public opinion that persons whose lack of responsibility and understanding had brought them under statutory care should pay the supreme penalty even for deliberate wickedness. There was much in Straffen's story to support the view expressed by Dr Leitch in the witness-box that 'the majority of children of nine-and-a-half years would show more ability to learn from experience, and to foresee the results of their acts, and would show more appreciation of right and wrong than he did'. Consider, for example, his reckless self-incriminatory interviews with the police, also the fact that, although his escape was carefully plotted, yet he had not provided himself with any money and had not arranged for any outside 'contacts' to shelter him. What had he proposed to do? He told one of the psychiatrists who examined him that he had meant to go to Manchester (to the police he had said Winchester), which he only knew as 'a big town a long way off where the police couldn't find him'. What did he think would happen when he got on a bus or train with no money for his fare? Although desperately anxious to avoid recapture, he had openly lounged about Farley Hill village for about an hour, marking down a victim. But most fatuous of all was his conduct in asking for a drink at a house almost on the site of the murder; other criminals manufacture alibis – Straffen manufactured evidence.

The Home Secretary does does not give reasons for reprieves, but it is a reasonable supposition that he had some such consideration in mind.

Mental deficiency alone, it is fair to add, would not account for Straffen's behaviour, though it might influence the course his actions took. Serious crime of any sort is rare among the feeble-minded, although they show a good deal of petty delinquency if not well supervised and helped. But like normal people, though to a less extent, defectives differ among themselves and display great diversity of character and temperament. Straffen's complete lack of remorse and appalling inability to enter into the feelings of his victims or their relatives, which shocked even experienced prison medical officers, might be called a psychopathic trait, but that would not help us much, for no one has yet been clever enough to define a psychopath. He is certainly not among the 'affectionless criminals', of whom much has been written, for he gave evidence of steady affection for his mother and sisters. Apparently there was a deep-rooted incapacity to get into emotional contact with anyone outside his family, for he had never been known to have a friend of either sex. His only contacts with young girls had ended in quarrels and violence.

Coupled with this emotional blocking, one finds in Straffen's history an intense resentment against correction for any fault, especially if the punishment had the effect of taking, or threatening to take him away from home. Nothing very abnormal in that, it may be thought, but the chain of actions and reactions that resentment set up in Straffen are fortunately very unusual indeed. As he is exceptionally timid in spite of his strong build, his hostility is not shown to his superiors, but is masked under a pleasant, amenable bearing and only finds expression in vindictive violence against some creature who cannot retaliate, such as an animal or a child. Here a new element enters into the murky picture, for one may presume that Straffen would not have chosen the same method and the same type of victim on three successive occasions unless the act of strangling a little girl had given him some pleasure. One can only surmise that he derived from it some emotional gratification probably of a specifically sexual nature. Some very good judges of human nature who have been in contact with him think this was the predominant motive in his crimes, but that is doubtful; Straffen had never been a menace to little girls except when he had a grievance to revenge. It is a tragic picture of a feeble brain, swept by evil impulses of unusual strength and diversity, and lacking the mechanism – and perhaps the will – for control.

How does a man's mind get into such a dreadful mess? In Straffen's case there may be a simple organic explanation, for his encephalograph tracings are grossly abnormal and suggest an unrecognized attack of encephalitis in childhood, possibly (though there is no confirmatory evidence) associated with an attack of measles at the age of three. If so, the lad's responsibility for his delinquencies is – quite possibly – no greater than that of a paralytic's responsibility for his withered leg, for there is ample evidence that encephalitis plays strange tricks with character development. Other observers would place the blame on the criminal's environment and would look for frustrated affections, or terrifying experiences in childhood – or bad example and lack of moral teaching. Here again we have to retire baffled for lack of sufficient evidence. There is said to be a missing factor in every obscure murder case which would clear up the mystery if it were known and, if known, could be published! And this is probably as true where the mystery is one of character and motive as it is in mysteries of fact.

Can such tragedies be avoided by a wiser handling of difficult children? Straffen's story does not give us much encouragement to think so. Psychologists could point to at least two critical periods in his life when his state of mind could have been probed more deeply with profit: when he first came under a Child Guidance Clinic at eight, and when he lapsed into odd forms of delinquency at seventeen. But many defectives are mentally inaccessible to psychological aid from the beginning and, even if they are more able to cooperate, it would be futile to put forward as practicable any scheme for attempting the psychological treatment of every dull and delinquent boy. It may also be said that at all costs the boy should have been kept among his own family and not sent to an institution, but that is to be wise — if it is a wise theory — after the event. The very experienced education officers, magistrates, and mental experts who knew all the facts at that date judged differently.

FAMOUS TRIALS 7
OSCAR WILDE

H. Montgomery Hyde

1857

On the 18th of February 1895, four days after the opening of *The Importance of Being Earnest*, the Marquess of Queensberry deposited at the Albermarle Club a card on which was written: 'To Oscar Wilde posing as a somdomite.' This misspelt but calculated challenge sounded the bell for the first round in one of the most bizarre contests ever staged at Old Bailey.

The prosecution (for criminal libel) of the eccentric Queensberry had to be abandoned by Sir Edward Clarke, and the Crown then took action against Oscar Wilde. At his second trial he was convicted of gross indecency with male persons and imprisoned for two years with hard labour. He died in Paris, bankrupt, in 1900.

These cases were remarkable for the disgraceful evidence of public jubilation over the verdicts; for the insane antics of Queensberry on behalf of his son, Lord Alfred Douglas, the young poet; and for the absurd vanity of Wilde himself, who tripped flippantly into a fatal trap during Carson's pitiless and staggering cross-examination.